FINDING FORECLOSURES

An Insider's Guide
To Cashing In
on this
Hidden Market

- Revolutionary internet tools help you discover the best properties

- Get great deals at the pre-foreclosure stage

- Money-saving auction and negotiation strategies

- Don't miss out on the booming foreclosure market

Danielle Babb & Bill Nazur

Editorial director: Jere L. Calmes
Cover design: Desktop Miracles, Inc.
Design and composition: MillerWorks

This publication is designed to provide accurate and authoritative information in regard to the subject matter covered. It is sold with the understanding that the publisher is not engaged in rendering legal, accounting, or other professional services. If legal advice or other expert assistance is required, the services of a competent professional person should be sought.

Library of Congress Cataloging-in-Publication Data

Babb, Danielle.
Finding foreclosures : an insider's guide to cashing in on this hidden market / by Danielle Babb & Bill Nazur.
    p. cm.
Includes bibliographical references.
ISBN-13: 978-1-59918-131-8 (alk. paper)
ISBN-10: 1-59918-131-2 (alk. paper)
1. Real estate investment. 2. Foreclosure. I. Nazur, Bill. II. Title.

HD1382.5.B33 2007
332.63'24—dc22   2007016132

Printed in Canada

FOREWORD

Historically, investing in foreclosure properties has been a hidden market, the purview of a select group of real estate investors with insider connections within the industry. Foreclosure filings, though technically public record data in most states, were hidden deep in the archives of the county recorder's office or posted in obscure legal journals, making the records difficult to find.

A process regulated on a state-by-state basis, and prone to sudden and sometimes inexplicable changes, the notion of even figuring out how to buy a foreclosure property was overwhelming to someone unfamiliar with the procedures. And the traditional infrastructure set up to manage real estate transactions—the Realtor® and the mortgage banker—were ill-equipped to handle these nontraditional sales.

All of these factors put the first time homebuyer, a homeowner looking for a second property, or a new real estate investor looking to break into the foreclosure market at a distinct disadvantage.

The internet has changed all of this—dramatically and definitively—and "democratized" the foreclosure market. Today, 30 million people visit real estate web sites every month, looking to find their next home to purchase. Over three million of these visit www.realtytrac.com, where they search through nearly one million foreclosure and bank-owned homes.

If you, like these eager investors and home buyers, are interested in making your real estate fortune or buying your own little piece of the American dream, foreclosure properties can represent an excellent way to get started. But successfully investing in foreclosures requires education, diligence, a tolerance for risk, and a little luck.

Dani Babb and Bill Nazur have compiled an easy-to-use, informative road map to help people navigate the world of foreclosure investing. It explains the process and the terminology, discusses practical, real world considerations every investor needs to address, provides dozens of useful resources, and gives a wealth of information you need to succeed.

You now have the road map. The resources are a mouse-click away. Foreclosures are at their highest levels in years. The next step is up to you, if you have the courage to take it.

Bon voyage!

Rick Sharga
VP of Marketing
RealtyTrac Inc.

Check page 168 for a special offer from RealtyTrac!

CONTENTS

Contents

ACKNOWLEDGMENTS

Bill Nazur:

- Gaby Acuna for her friendship, support, and constant drive for excellence in everything that is real estate.
- Marco Marroquin and Ben Valenzuela, Jr., for helping expand my sphere of influence.
- Eric C. Nelson for teaching me everything on earth about underwriting.
- My wonderful co-author, client, and friend, Dani Babb, for being so casual, yet so driven at becoming the best.

Dani Babb:

- Rick Sharga and Jim Saccacio, for bringing fabulous tools to market and providing excellent advice and sound practice.
- Bill Nazur, for his friendship, his expertise, his persistence, and his patience.
- Jere Calmes, for his trust, support, and passion.
- Bob Diforio, without whom no deal would get done, no book sold, and no consumer educated.
- To my new friend Shane—thanks for making me laugh and for challenging everything.
- Alex Lazo, for his friendship, depth, and daily humor—without him, I would have gone insane three years ago!

DEDICATION

To my beautiful wife and wonderful family,
who serve as the foundation and motivation
for always raising the bar higher.
—Bill Nazur

To my supportive husband; his respect for
my work, his encouragement, and his unwavering
selflessness to let me be myself and
kick some you-know-what.
—Dani Babb

INTRODUCTION

Every year, over eight million homeowners look for help to prevent the foreclosure of a home that they own. It is estimated that 2007 will see an astounding 12 million foreclosures across the U.S. Of these individuals, many will, in fact, have their homes taken back by the bank in a process called foreclosure where, basically, the bank (due to default on a mortgage or note) sells the property to pay off the lien against the home. While this is unfortunate for those homeowners, it presents incredible opportunity to those interested in buying a home in an area they thought they could never afford, or an investor looking for some pocket change. By the time you finish this book, you will have the information necessary to take advantage of this equity opportunity.

Before the internet and some great online companies, only those "in the know" could buy foreclosures—in fact, finding them was downright impossible and almost maddening. With today's tools, the playing field is leveled and now is the time to take advantage of it. In 2006, the Center for Responsible Lending predicted that one in every five sub-prime mortgages that originated in the previous two years would end up in foreclosure. One in five—20 percent—a staggering number (Carter, 2006). The risk is so great in fact that nearly half the states—19 plus the District of Columbia—adopted tighter guidelines for underwriting and disclosing the terms of "exotic" mortgages. If you think the exotic mortgages shouldn't be a concern, then you have not read the latest news from the Mortgage Bankers Association that indicates that $1.1 trillion to $1.7 trillion of adjustable rate mortgages may reset in 2007. Of those, $600 billion to $700 billion will refinance before they reset. Included in this requirement is the need to prove that the homeowner can pay a fully indexed, fully amortized rate—a worst case scenario. This is assuming that they have the available credit and equity to allow this to happen. Additionally, the same organization has shown that the remaining $500 billion to $800 billion will reset. This is only for the current year. There will be many homeowners though for many years to come (and many states that refuse the new laws) that will not be able to make their payments. This is where you step in, presuming that you take the time to prepare yourself appropriately. Start reading, and we'll walk you through the steps.

Why Foreclosures, and Why Now?

Last year, the hot book topics in real estate were on house flipping, investing for idiots, and buying up real estate "like a pro." In the future, the focus will be on what to do with your newfound troubled credit score, your immense debt, and your undervalued home. The best of them all? Foreclosures, which represent an incredible potential gain for those willing to invest some time and money and put technology to work for them, will allow individuals with the knowledge and wherewithal to begin their real estate investment portfolio at a discount.

Many factors are contributing to the incredible rise in the number of foreclosures as well as the predicted increase. For starters, many people didn't understand the ramifications of the most popular form of financing seen in decades—a negative amortization loan. They knew they wanted a nice house, the market was rising, and people were afraid if they "didn't buy now, they never could." They took loans that were cheap in the beginning with so-called introductory one-month teaser rates, that beginning in the second month suddenly shot up to a fully indexed rate, leaving unsuspecting homeowners unable to pay bills. We've only seen the beginning of this particular contributing factor. What else is causing issues? Some experts say rising insurance rates, rising flood premiums, and increases in property and supplemental taxes are also part of the cause (by the way, all things to watch out for when buying foreclosures too!). We'll explain more moving forward.

Buyers were in a frenzy to purchase, resulting in overpaying for homes, driving market value increases that were unsustainable beyond a couple of months, let alone years. Some creative investors even created markets by buying up property in an area, getting their clients to invest in it, and then dumping it when the market shot up, only to leave the rest of the investors with undervalued property and high loans. Builders are being sued in class action suits and individuals are losing their homes. Regrettably, any hot market, whether real estate, stocks, or other investments, bring out the crooked people as well as the honest ones.

Some lost equity due to a downturn in the market and poor market conditions, with over-inflated areas, especially in some specific markets like Florida, tanking. Others in California and the coastal states looked at their homes as piggy banks, sucking every penny out of their homes— using their home equity lines of credit (HELOC) as credit cards to purchase motorcycles, watercraft, and exotic vehicles, all of which quickly depreciate. If the same cash would have been used for investment purposes with a high level of understanding, few people would be impacted; however, too many people gambled and lost.

It is interesting to both of us that people attempt to downplay the financial severity of what is happening. We know that from a percentage standpoint, foreclosures represent a small amount of our overall gross domestic product, but when you are looking at the raw dollars in the billions, how could you not see the opportunity for tremendous gains? It is time to look at the root causes, and make some financial moves that will afford each of us a solid investment in real estate whether we decide to live in the home, or begin a portfolio of rentals. Let's keep looking at what is occurring so you know how to take advantage of this change within the marketplace.

Lots of people going into foreclosure had marital woes, medical issues, job loss, or had to take pay cuts to help their companies avoid bankruptcy. Some simply couldn't hold onto their second homes or investment properties due to interest rate increases and since it is "better" to lose a house you do not live in than one you do, they let the investments go back to the bank. Not always a wise option looking backward, but an option nonetheless. It is said that hindsight is 20/20. We'll help you look forward to spot the opportunities in the coming years.

Slowing of the real estate market into 2007 and beyond indicates that high inventory levels, downward pricing trends, higher mortgage rates, and foreclosure rates are all indicative of the potential for greater foreclosure opportunities in the future. In 2005 alone, the number of foreclosures went up nationwide by 24.5 percent (Rihn, 2006). Some areas have seen more staggering numbers than others. For instance, as reported by CBS News, Weld County, Colorado, was one of the hottest housing markets in the country—until 2004. You could hear the slamming of the brakes on market value. In this area, like several others, "Home buyers with adjustable rate mortgages faced payments they couldn't afford. Those forced to sell couldn't find buyers and hundreds defaulted on their loans. Now the place leads the nation in foreclosures—1 in every 168 households—700 percent higher than the national average" (Alfonsi, 2006). While some blame the federal open market committee, commonly referred to as "the Fed," for the interest rate hike, others argue it was necessary to stave off inflation—one thing is for sure, and that is foreclosures will become more common as the days go on and more adjustable rate mortgages do precisely that—adjust. Nationwide, more than 300,000 properties in 2006 entered foreclosure just during the third quarter alone; 43 percent more than from one year ago. If you think this trend will change for the positive, think again. It has gotten worse, and will continue to worsen in the coming months and years. More loans that had three or five-year flat rates will adjust soon, increasing this further. "Somewhere between 1.2 million and 1.3 million properties will end up in some state of foreclosure over the course of 2006" (Sharga, 2006). "Things got so bad in Colorado that the state set up the first-of-its-kind foreclosure help hotline and it got 1,400 calls on the first day" (Alfonsi,

2006). Currently, there is about a trillion dollars in adjustable rate mortgages that will "reset" over the next 15 months (Sharga, 2006). (Note: This was in October of 2006!) "The average homeowner will see an increase of between 20 and 50 percent of their monthly mortgage bill" (Sharga, 2006). Average, of course, means precisely that—some will see an even greater increase. This could cause many homeowners who bought with no down payment or who bought interest-only or negative amortization loans to go into default. Another downside to foreclosing (besides the obvious) is that if a neighbor defaults, a home next door will drop in value by about $10,000. The number of foreclosures in California has tripled since 2005, and Colorado, Nevada, and Florida lead the nation with the highest foreclosure rates.

While this is burdensome and difficult for those who lose their homes, it is an incredible opportunity for those who wish to increase the holdings in their portfolios or make money in the foreclosure market. We strongly believe anyone in the position of possible foreclosure should do everything possible to save their home, pay back their obligation, get creative, and keep themselves out of financial ruin. But in many cases, the owner does not want to do so or is so far upside down that they view their situation as being impossible. We'll even talk about how you can get to some of these individuals in a way that benefits the owner, and you, the investor.

In this book, Bill Nazur, mortgage banker, and Danielle Babb, professor and investor, tell you how to cash in on the opportunities foreclosures have begun to create. These opportunities will continue to grow exponentially in the coming years, especially as interest-only loans end their initial fixed term and negative amortization loans fully amortize, causing individuals to find it tough to pay their mortgages. Step by step, the authors walk you through foreclosures, the process, how to buy, what to look for, the pitfalls to avoid, financing, and what to do with the property once you own it. We also tell you which site, after reviewing many, we feel is *the* site to use to find foreclosures, and why. This one-stop guide will explain everything you need to know to *start making money in foreclosures*.

CHAPTER ONE

WHAT IS A FORECLOSURE?

MOST OF US ASSOCIATE FORECLOSURES WITH A TERRIBLE TRAGEDY— a family being forced to move, a person having bad credit history for at least seven years, and the need to 'start again' from the ground up. This is partly true for some, but a foreclosure also represents an incredible opportunity to live in an area you never dreamed possible, or begin your investment portfolio with a solid equity position. This equity position is what we'll explore, and exploit, so you can begin down the path of foreclosure investment and ownership.

So, what is a foreclosure exactly? Simply stated, a foreclosure is the lender-initiated legal process or court action that occurs when a borrower fails to comply with terms and conditions in a loan. The process is a combination of state and federal laws, so the length of time for a foreclosure to happen will vary significantly from state to state. Often, this occurs because the bank needs to repay a lien on a home and the only way to do that is for the bank to take the property and sell it. In a foreclosure, the borrower has no rights, title, or interest in the property and the mortgaged property is sold to pay the loan of the borrower that has defaulted. In some states, a foreclosure can occur to pay other debt that is secured by a home, even if the loan in default isn't for that particular property. We'll start off with some interesting and important facts, and then explain why they are relevant.

Interesting Facts

As reported in a memo titled "A Confused Real Estate Market" issued by Fidelity Residential Solutions in 2006, the following facts are documented:

- Florida has the highest current foreclosure rate and held 14 percent of the nation's foreclosures in 2005—1.67 percent of the state's homes in 2005 were in foreclosure.

Foreclosures are a tragedy to some; they are an opportunity for others. It's important to understand what creates both situations.

- Colorado's foreclosure rate ranks second in the nation—1.62 percent of the state's homes.
- Utah has the third highest foreclosure rate at 1.5 percent of the state's homes in foreclosure.
- Texas foreclosures increased 54 percent in 2005 from the first quarter to the fourth.
- The past few years have resulted in historically low interest rates.
- We've seen strong employment figures in the past few years.
- Home prices have seen record highs.
- Steadily increasing interest rates and decreasing home prices will always result in higher numbers of foreclosures.

Common Reasons for Foreclosure

Foreclosure can happen to just about anyone; job loss, the end of marital bliss, excess debt, or decreasing income are all catalysts. Recently, a couple of other reasons have become more prevalent—homes financed at 100 percent of their equity without the ability to repay or a credit profile to support such a transaction; or individuals making payments of less than the interest on their home and not having enough equity to refinance when their payments become higher. (We will go into this in far more detail later.) Missed tax payments, missed mortgage payments, divorce, job loss, and illness are still the most frequently seen causes of foreclosure, often reasons that are not within the control of the individual losing his or her home.

Market conditions also can contribute to a greater number of foreclosures. Inflated real estate prices can create situations where buyers are overpaying for homes, then a sudden drop in the price makes it difficult, if not impossible, to sell the property. One of the co-authors of this book is in the process of purchasing a home that appraised significantly below the purchase price. The builder "recommended" that a mortgage note for the difference should be signed, creating an environment that lends itself to paying over the purchase price, and creating a higher propensity to default in the future, as the market would not help recover the difference for at least 3-5 years at best. You can imagine this didn't go over well. You know you love the home, and for a split second your might consider this kind of commitment. But you need to realize that down the line, you cannot do this without gigantic risk to your personal financial position.

Often, when an investor or homeowner can no longer afford the payment, he or she will "ride out the market" by renting out the property until the home is valuable again. The problem with this approach is that when interest rates are cheap, the number of potential renters often decreases because those renters can now afford to buy homes. This is an acceptable approach to borrowers that can carry the additional debt while the market improves, or more favorable financing comes along based on the equity position of the home.

Increasing equity line interest rates can really hurt cash flow for families, also leading to more foreclosures. You can be wealthy and still struggle month-to--month due to cash flow, so do not underestimate the quality of homes that can go into foreclosure. Additionally, 90 to 100 percent loan-to-value financing can create stressful situations whereby individuals cannot tap equity to make mortgage payments, due to the ebb and flow of market values.

Another common reason leading to a greater quantity of foreclosures is 100 percent financing on second homes and investment properties. The most innocent and well-intentioned people can be drawn into real estate with a complete reliance on continued appreciation and without a true understanding of the cash flow required to maintain the payments on property in addition to those on their primary residence, their vehicles, and all of their other consumer goodies. Incidentally, in 2005, 25 percent of the homes sold were to investors, some of which accumulated a great level of wealth—and some of which are now going into foreclosure, creating an opportunity for the next wave of buyers. Human behavior and, frankly, common sense, dictates that if someone is having difficulty paying their mortgage, they will not pay their investment property payments before their primary home, leading to greater risk for the bank and greater default rates for investment properties. Historically, this has been the case, and will continue in the coming years. While many second homes are truly investment properties, these properties are currently priced and underwritten to the same standard as an owner-occupied home and are not yet charged a higher interest rate, yet the performance on the payment of these assets is below that of the primary home portfolio across the U.S.

Last but certainly not least, the interest-only and negative-amortization loans will approach the maximum loan-to-value cap and automatically readjust. This will cause the owner's payments to increase tremendously, as the mortgage company wants the remaining balance paid off within the remaining years of the term. For example, if you defer interest and reach your cap in four years, a loan for 30 years will now require principal and interest payment due and payable monthly but amortized over 26 years instead of 30. This does not make for an attractive payment, leaving the buyer with much higher payments and less equity in their home as they continue to defer interest in exchange for a lower monthly payment.

A recent introduction of 40-year and even 50-year mortgages helps cover the spread on the recalculation of the remaining term, but this only applies once your initial interest-only period is over. As an investor, does it make sense to work with a 40- or 50-year term? Typically no, unless you have the ability to enter into an "option ARM," which allows you to keep the ability to make higher payments when possible without deferring interest. You must also be gaining equity faster than you're adding to your balance!

What Happens When a Home is Foreclosed On?

Both the homeowner and the investor wanting to buy a distressed property need to understand how the process of foreclosure works, to know when to intervene, when to make decisions, and how to facilitate a smooth process and transition. According to Century 21, the foreclosure procedure generally begins after three months of missed payments. But in Georgia, for example, the foreclosure procedure starts after 37 days!

In a nutshell, the lender records a notice of default against the property. Unless payments are made, the property goes to a trustee sale, which sells the property to the highest bidder. Of course, this is overly simplified and we will illustrate the time lines later.

The foreclosure process commonly ends in one of four ways:

1. The borrower reinstates the loan by paying off the amount owed during a grace period determined by law.

2. The borrower sells the property to a third party during the pre-foreclosure period.

3. A third party takes the property at a public auction.

4. The lender takes ownership of the home with the intent to resell it.

The bank may, in fact, actually buy the property at the public auction. These bank-owned homes are also called REOs or Real Estate Owned. These homes, typically in the "fixer-upper" stage, can serve as great investment opportunities. For example, RealtyTrac provides a centralized platform for researching foreclosure properties at various stages in the process. A recent search of RealtyTrac indicated over 900,000 homes available across the U.S. A subsequent search minutes later showed that a prime lender such as Bank of America shows 268 bank-owned properties, also across the U.S. One item that stands out in this snapshot analysis when searching for a foreclosure is that the prime lenders who have the most stringent underwriting standards will have the lowest amount of properties available for sale, while a sub-prime lender, such as an Ameriquest or New Century, who have looser or more liberal underwriting standards, will have a greater quantity of available properties for sale. As a matter of public record, the latter of these companies, New Century, recently lost over 25 percent of their market value, resulting in a loss of billions of dollars on Wall Street due to the poor performance of several assets that had to be re-purchased by the mortgage company for their early payment defaults. This example may be merely the tip of the iceberg, so if you choose to research independently, keep this in mind.

The internet is a powerful tool that helps level the playing field of foreclosure research. We believe that one should approach foreclosures from a position of strength when it comes to research and knowledge. Use the internet for maximum efficiency—or you can review your local newspaper, take notes, make some phone calls, leave some messages, follow up repeatedly, and HOPE that something happens. Indeed, something will happen; you will drive yourself nuts as the homes will most likely be sold to someone else more savvy who decided to use technology to help them. Preparation is key; financial commitment is critical; action is imperative. However, also bear in mind that if you over-analyze the situation, the opportunity to purchase the foreclosure may quickly disappear.

If you want to buy a home with pre-foreclosure status, you must approach the borrower or homeowner with an agreement to buy it. At this point, the seller is already behind in their payments; this should be the time frame where the owner is most accommodating and willing to work with an "angel" buyer. Since the seller is not yet desperate to unload the property, you may experience some resistance. This pre-foreclosure type of sale is referred to as a For Sale By Owner (FSBO) transaction, though often a real estate agent may be involved. The buyer is given the time to research the title and condition of the property, but often these homes sell for 20 to 40 percent below market value. Again, the seller wants to cut his or her losses by selling the home, but still maintain some equity if at all possible. This truly does become a "win-win" scenario—you can purchase a home for below market value and the seller can maintain their dignity and walk away with some small amount of equity. This is truly the ideal situation where both parties stand to benefit.

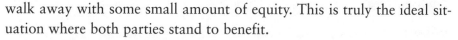

Foreclosure timeline varies from as little as 37 days up to 6 months, depending on the state. Learn the state and federal laws that apply to you, as they serve as a protection to the bank, as well as to the homeowner and to the investor looking to purchase.

A word of caution, however: If you try to drive a hard bargain as an investor, you will certainly frustrate your seller and perhaps lose the deal. Human nature just does not allow us to believe we should leave anything on the table, particularly when it comes to money. Behavior in this instance is not always rational. You are walking into the situation as a mediator, and helping solve a problem that benefits you as an investor or buyer.

If the loan isn't reinstated by the end of the pre-foreclosure period, the property goes to auction where buyers are often required to pay in cash. Each auction has different rules that you need to research before you decide to participate. Initial deposits will vary greatly between companies, as well as from state to state. This process does not allow for much time to research the property beforehand; however, these often produce the best bargains and they avoid dealing with the emotionally involved owner of the property and the difficulties that can create. If you have the available capital, or pool of capital, prepare yourself as this is a great opportunity for a substantial equity position. Just like the stock market, you want to buy low and sell high. While foreclosures are constant, today's market is very much the ideal market to do this in. The next few years will be filled with more opportunities to tap into this market than we've seen over the last few years.

If the lender does take ownership of the property, they will want to resell the property to pay off the lien(s), as the interest will continue to accumulate until the property is sold, and taken off the books. As banks do not like delinquent accounts on their books, they will generally clear titles and at times perform maintenance and repair. The profit for buyers and investors in these homes is often less than in pre-foreclosure homes, although they still

Finding the facts

In the time it took to write this manuscript, Ameriquest shut down its retail lending operations, and New Century Mortgage had filed for bankruptcy. This job reduction affected over 5,800 employees at the two companies alone. The housing-related industries lost over 176,000 jobs in the year-over-year comparisons for the quarter ending March '07, according to figures compiled by Moodys.com.

represent a worthy investment. If the loan is backed by a government agency such as HUD or the Department of Veterans Affairs (VA), the government agency is responsible for selling the property so you would, in those cases, deal with these lenders instead of a traditional bank (RealtyTrac, 2006).

Timelines

So how long does it take to go through each step of the foreclosure process? The answer is "it depends." It depends on how the homeowner responds to the bank's inquiries, to the repayment strategies the bank offers, or what assistance the homeowner seeks. It further depends on the state in which you live in, as well as that of the lender carrying the mortgage that is being foreclosed upon. Lenders' loss mitigation departments will not begin the foreclosure process until they feel that all opportunities to negotiate with the current owner are exhausted. Having said that, we will discuss examples in two states that, due to value and overall population, tend to have a large amount of foreclosures in absolute numbers, though not necessarily as a percentage of overall resale activity.

In California, for example, after missing three consecutive payments, the foreclosure timeline begins immediately. While still empathetic to the entire process and the impact on the individual or family that is being foreclosed on, my experience shows that the current owner of the residence has been contacted numerous times by phone and mail. More than sufficient notice is typically provided, allowing the buyer several opportunities to respond. Unlike a missed credit card payment, this is a far more serious matter. Usually the pre-lien period is 30 days, followed by the lien period, which will take another 30 days. At this point, the collection or loss mitigation departments will work with the borrower to prevent the process from moving forward. The bank or servicing group is still your ally during this stage. Kindness on the bank's part should not be mistaken for weakness, as they are building a case against the borrower if they fail to respond or make arrangements to catch up on payments. As a buyer, you could purchase the home with immediate equity by assisting the borrower through what is about to become a horrible ordeal. After three months, a notice of default is filed and within 21 to 25 days after that, a notice of sale is filed. Once the notice of default has been filed, the clock is ticking quickly and loudly. The owner can still cure the default by bringing payments current, which in certain circumstances they will. Depending on the equity in the home, "hard money" or private lenders will step in to help with above market interest rates. To insulate the investor against potential loss, as they are placing money against a risky borrower, they will not lend on any property with a loan-to-value over 65 percent. In case there is no other solution, the property then goes to a Trustee sale, and if it remains unsold, it becomes an REO. Most homes are sold in the Trustee sale phase, so as an investor, you need to plan accordingly and act quickly. Essentially, in California, you are looking at a total of 180 days from the beginning of the process to the very end.

In Texas, however, the entire process may only take 60 days (www.foreclosurelaw.org). As the market continues to contract, one can expect each lender to become more aggressive in initiating the foreclosure process more efficiently, while at the same time creating a clogged pipeline of real estate that they really have no interest in owning. This may serve to create a greater desire to negotiate down the price, therefore creating greater values for buyers and investors; it may merely extend the length of time that it will take to complete the process with a flattening of prices as the banks will need to mitigate their potential losses further.

State-Dependent Actions

There are two types of proceedings that can occur on foreclosure property. One is called judicial and the other is non-judicial. In states that require the process be judicial, the entire proceeding is conducted through the courts. This is a far more complicated process, and like any other process that must go through the courts, will carry costs and risks that can just as easily be resolved without the supervision of the courts. Some states, such as Alabama, Michigan, and Texas, do allow both but in general, each state has a method that is most common for its residents. In states that do allow both, the mortgage security itself dictates how proceedings will occur. A deed of trust often allows for non-judicial proceedings, while mortgages allow for judicial foreclosures. However, some mortgages do specifically state the allowance for procedure without judicial intervention.

Foreclosures occur at all levels, from starter homes to million dollar mansions. The cash-flow issues that often impact individuals or families going into foreclosure can be the a result of a simple job loss or a catastrophic business slowdown. Not many people are immune.

In states that follow a judicial practice, lenders must file paperwork with the court against the owner if he/she is in default. If the court rules against the owner, the home is quickly put up for sale to the public. Since each state has specific laws, we recommend that you review the laws by state at www.RealtyTrac.com/education/noframes/foreclosurePro.html. Make sure you are thoroughly familiar with the rules in the state you're working in. An additional resource is www.foreclosurelaw.org. Their data is constantly changing, so this particular web site requires frequent visits. Don't bother printing out their information as it becomes obsolete quickly.

We can write an entire book on the actual proceedings as they relate to each state. Much of that information is already available online, particularly by researching this data in Google or Yahoo Search!

THE CREATIVE LOAN ERA

THE LAST DECADE HAS PRODUCED AN ENTIRELY NEW ERA OF LOANS. No so long ago, the purchase agreement for property was typically one to three pages, and the mortgage choices were a 30-year fixed with 20 percent down, FHA with 3 percent down, or VA financing with no money down if you had your honorable discharge, (DD-214 in government terms). Fast forward a few years and your typical mortgage averages 75 pages minimum, per mortgage, and while those earlier lending instruments still exist, they represent a far smaller portion of the market than ever before. Ah, the good old days. Well, they're gone, and the banks as well as the market seem to have adapted.

With historically low interest rates, a strong demand for housing, and a generally strong economy, lenders found all types of creative ways to compete for business. The creativity is certainly far from over, though credit scoring and overall qualifications are more important than ever. As we move forward, you will continue to see credit tightening as it relates to quality of lending, verification of assets, and various other factors related to the overall creativity in the marketplace. With consumer confidence in the market, high appraisals (some say too high), and a generally inflated market, many people purchased homes that they couldn't afford on a monthly cash flow basis determined using creative financing, all perfectly allowed and encouraged by lenders. Generally speaking, a high credit score and a little bit of equity in a home and lenders would provide financing at astoundingly low rates.

Interestingly, credit scoring has become so statistically accurate and relevant that credit history combined with a FICO score is highly predictive of default. So while lenders understand that a 640 FICO score is within the range of the national average, historical performance of the score itself indicates that you will have a higher propensity of default within a specific period of time. The same is true of a credit score one hundred points higher, representing a far lower propensity to default, along with a credit score one hundred points lower, representing a significantly higher propensity to default. Additionally, there are software products that predict the performance of the servicing portfolio for the mortgage company, as well as loss mitigation software that helps manage the default process (BackinTheBlack,® 2005). As a buyer and/or investor, it is beneficial to understand the mechanics behind the behavior that ultimately resorts in your individual ability to get involved in the business of foreclosure investing. This knowledge will help you greatly when you begin investing in the business of foreclosures.

The Fixed-Rate Mortgage

In previous generations, the only loan option was the fixed-rate mortgage, whether it was conventional, or one of the government versions of Federal Housing Authority (FHA) and the Veterans Administration (VA) loan programs. Investors call this a "rip off" because essentially the homeowner has to pay the bank a combination of principal and interest, resulting in the eventual outright ownership of the home after 30 years— money they could invest in other properties, stocks, bonds, or other more lucrative investments for a substantially greater gain.

In the Baby Boomer generation, we can say it was a worthy decision. Dani keeps hearing the words of her parents and grandparents cautioning against her "creative financing" and the risk she's taking by not owning a home when she retires. Different generations, as well as different cultures, have a different take on their investment methods. Even today, some prefer this route and feel it is a safer bet over the long term. Individuals who choose this loan type often choose a 15- or 30-year fixed-rate mortgage, meaning that the rate for the loan as well as the terms are fixed for the entire period. A certain benefit to this loan type is that rarely do individuals get themselves in over their heads, as they are only buying as much home as they can afford. There is a definite benefit to the fixed-rate program, dating back to the considerably lower purchase prices of the past, that has allowed 30 percent of homeowners across the U.S to not have a mortgage at all (Watts, Gary 2007 speech). But the prices today really make this difficult.

Conversely, a downside to a fixed-rate mortgage is that it is an expensive insurance policy against the possibility of rates rising in the future. Bill is a firm believer in making sure all assets are adequately insured—and perhaps over-insured—but still does not believe that a 30-year fixed-rate loan makes much financial sense in most situations. Dani believes it is a waste of money that could be invested for greater gain, provides a lack of flexibility in payments if cash flow is tight, and of course presents the need to refinance regularly if interest rates drop. The big downside to having flexibility, however, is that this type of loan costs more compared to other types of loans. We will get to the other options we both refer to here later in this chapter.

> Fixed-rate loans are an expensive insurance policy to protect against future market changes, unless you KNOW that you will stay in the home long term. The average homeowner moves every five to seven years.

Finding the facts

The rate of appreciation has been so strong in recent times that it would be wise to do a decade-to-decade comparison. As noted by Dr. Steve Sjuggerud in The Investment U e-Letter, "In Florida, if you bought a home in 1976, you did not break even until 2001, when you account for the effects of inflation." We can see what happened after 2001! House prices began to rise sharply, then drop off dramatically, which led to a very large default rate and an incredibly high rate of inventory—which naturally lowers prices to bring the market back to equilibrium.

Nationally, going all the way back to the 1960s, home prices have risen about 6 percent, to quote the same source. Inflation has risen on average of 4 percent, meaning real estate has really only appreciated 2 percent per year after inflation—until the 2000s. This statistical data should illustrate that one must be prepared for a worst-case scenario as well when looking at a real estate purchase, due to the potential volatility across various markets. This incredible boom in value over the last several years however, also means impending doom—which is where you can cash in.

Author's Notes

Each hot region over time has experienced big booms and big busts. California, Hawaii, and Florida have all experienced both throughout history. The key to any type of investing is buying low and selling high. Foreclosures give you an opportunity to buy low even when the selling is moderately high in resale homes or new construction.

Real estate truly is local. For this reason alone, one should be cautious when reading the newspapers or listening to the evening news, as the statistical data is generally national or regional and fails to look at a specific local market. As I have indicated to so many clients, you are being provided with 30 seconds worth of knowledge when you rely on news outlets for guidance in real estate investing. Let's look at Dr. Sjuggerud's findings again. In Iowa in 1980, prices fell 15 percent. Farmers left due to bad weather and high interest rates. Many people filed for bankruptcy, yet our traditionally hot markets were untouched. Real estate is local regardless of whether or not you're buying a resale home, a new build, or a foreclosure. A foreclosure in a terrible area just leaves you with an undervalued house that will be hard to sell in the same bad area. This is a critical reason for conducting your research in advance.

Comparatively speaking, housing is cheap. If we look at the Housing Affordability Index (which takes into consideration mortgage payments, incomes, and home prices) we are at early 1970s levels for price. People tend to manage the mortgage payment, not the purchase price. This is but one of many reasons it is so important to keep interest rates low. There is great information on housing affordability indexes that you can access at www. realtor.org/Research.nsf/ Pages/HousingInx.

Another upside to the traditional loan is that equity is apparent; since the equity is the home's value minus simply the loan balance, it is relatively easy to take out a line of credit or a second mortgage should the need arise. However, if you are an investor, it may be difficult to have positive cash flow on a rental property under this model, whereby most investors count on appreciation, not paying down the balance of the loan, for real gain. Most investors want maximum leverage; a fixed-rate mortgage is not the way to do that. Fixed-rate mortgages in general are more difficult to qualify for and they require higher credit scores and greater equity position. If, however, there is a marginal credit record, an underwriter may recommend a fixed-rate mortgage as it provides a level of comfort to the lending institution by reducing exposure to the lender. As a client you may not like it, but it could also be the only way to qualify. Fortunately, most fixed-rate mortgages rarely carry a prepayment penalty, so you could get out of the loan at any time by refinancing into more creative financing six months into the loan.

Having pointed out some of the advantages and disadvantages of a 30-year fixed rate, there are some similarities and differences on a 20-year, or even a 15-year fixed-rate mortgage. While a 15-year mortgage does not do much to help one's cash flow, it is an excellent financial instrument, assuming that all of your other investments are properly funded. For example, on a 30-year fixed-rate mortgage at 6.00 percent with a balance of $500,000, you can expect to pay an additional $578,000 in interest in addition to the $500,000 principal that you need to pay down; so yes, that $500,000 home will cost you over a million dollars before all is said and done. The same home on a 15-year mortgage with the same balance, at a lower rate of 5.75 percent will only cost you an additional $247,000 in interest. If you could purchase some foreclosure properties with a sufficient down payment and a combination of a below market purchase, you could place the home on a shorter term that could have a positive cash flow. If the tenant is paying the mortgage AND you can save some mortgage interest, a shorter term may make excellent financial sense.

Of course, the 30-year mortgage is the past. Moving forward, you will begin to see 40- year, and even 50-year mortgages as houses are simply too expensive to amortize over 30 years in the absence of a significant down payment. Add to that fact that people are living longer, combined with the changing demographic that has dual or multiple generations buying a home as a collective unit. Fixed-rate options will exist, though not even as prevalent as today. We will discuss this topic later in greater detail.

The Adjustable Rate Mortgage (ARM) and Interest-Only Loans

Adjustable rate mortgages became more popular as interest rates decreased. Individuals wanted to take advantage of the low interest rates that were set for a period of three to seven years, and then changed based on the current market condition after that time. During the last eight years, clients that had these loans actually saw their loans move downward at times with the rate decreases coming from the capital markets. ARMs adjust up or down at specified intervals, which can be yearly or after several years. They are commonly referred to by the length of the initial term, followed by the frequency of change in the rate. For example, a 5/1 is fixed for the first five years, with a subsequent rate change each year after that. The typical lifetime increase is 5 percent over the note rate, with a maximum first-year increase of 2 percent per year. This means that in a worst case scenario, the rate could increase 2 percent at the beginning of year six, an identical increase of 2 percent at the beginning of year seven, and only a 1 percent increase at the beginning of the seventh year when you reach your rate ceiling. Rates do have the ability to decrease in the same increments, subject to a rate floor that is specified when signing the mortgage note.

One major benefit to ARMs is that the initial interest rate that the homebuyer has to pay is usually substantially lower than that of a fixed-rate mortgage, making it easier to qualify for the loan and easier to get used to making bigger payments. These programs come in the form of fully amortizing loans that also pay down principal each month, as well as interest-only loans that cover the interest spread only without a reduction of principal each month. (Of course, you can still choose to pay principal payments, but why not invest that in something else?) At the end of the initial period, the rate is recalculated based on the margin and index so that the balance can be paid during the remainder of the term. For example, if the rate is fixed for the first five years of a 30-year loan, the recalculation is designed to show that the mortgage will need to be paid during the remaining 25 years. This is a good choice for people who do not plan to stay in their home beyond the fixed period of the loan because they are paying minimal interest to the bank and can use the money to save for other purposes or diversify in other investments.

As with any other mortgage, you can pay additional money towards principal should you wish. As mentioned in the example, ARMs are generally categorized as 1/1, 3/1, 5/1, 7/1, and 10/1 meaning that the initial fixed rate period is one, three, five seven, or ten years, with rates adjusting on an annual basis afterwards. This is a good option if you want to pay a lower payment while renting out a home and you do not intend to hold the property long, or you expect to be making substantially more money in the future (Metrocities). These programs are also great cash-flow tools that allow you to have a set minimum payment of interest only, where you would have the option of applying additional money against principal when bonuses or extra money comes in, while still allowing you to pare back in the instance you could not pay additional money against your payment. As an investor, this is a great tool to use when buying foreclosure properties, as the first few years of any loan are designed to cover more interest than anything else.

Conventional Mortgages

Loans that are insured by the government and for amounts within limits that are established by Fannie Mae and Freddie Mac (government-regulated private companies) are considered conventional mortgages. These loans are administered by the two agencies and there is a cap on the amount of money a conventional mortgage can lend. In the United States, this cap is $417,000 for single-family residences, two-unit loans at $533,850, three-unit loans at $645,300, and four-unit loans at $801,950. The maximum amounts for one to four family mortgages in Alaska, Hawaii, Guam, and the U.S. Virgin Islands are 50 percent higher than the limits for the rest of the country (Fannie Mae, 2007). Nonconventional mortgages, sometimes referred to as "jumbo" mortgages (see below), often result in a higher yield or interest rate, or different (stricter) terms and conditions. (Metrocities).

Jumbo Loans

Jumbo loans exceed the conventional amount for a loan noted above. This simply means that the mortgage is funded by a private investor or the private investment market. Note that if a loan is a jumbo loan, it is by definition nonconventional (Metrocities). Jumbo loans often have different requirements than conventional loans because they are funding homes of higher value, albeit often times with greater down payments as well, which can still pose a greater risk for the bank because the payments are higher.

Federal Housing Authority (FHA) Loans

The Federal Housing Authority does not fund loans, they merely insure them. These loans were initially designed for low- and middle-income borrowers and first-time homeowners. They tend to be easier to qualify for than conventional loans (Metrocities). The most widely used FHA loan is the Fixed Rate 203(b) loan. According to vamortgagecenter.com, some of the important issues you should know regarding fixed-rate loans are:

- You choose a period of time in which you want to pay back your loan, which can be 15, 20, or 30 years. Keep in mind that interest rates are usually lower on mortgages that are for shorter periods of time, but your monthly payments are lower on mortgages that are for longer periods of time.

- Your interest rate is higher than adjustable rate mortgages because the interest rate will stay the same throughout the lifetime of your loan.
- Your payments will be fixed and never increase with the exception of property tax increases and homeowner's insurance increases, which may cause your payments to rise slightly.
- Fixed-rate mortgages are a good choice for people who plan to stay in their new home for more than five years and build equity.

As you can see, the benefits mentioned on an FHA loan mirror those of a conventional fixed-rate mortgage. Aside from overall credit criteria, and the usage of Private Mortgage Insurance (PMI), an FHA fixed-rate loan only requires a minimum 3 percent down payment. In addition, the FHA may introduce a no-money down loan sometime in 2007 or 2008. While these loans require a complete verification of income and assets, this is an easy loan to qualify for throughout the U.S., though is not commonly used in higher value markets such as California.

FHA Secured Loans

Another type of FHA loan to consider is the adjustable rate loan, which many people are unaware of. This loan will give you a lower interest rate than traditional fixed-rate loans initially, such as 3, 5, or 7 years. After that, the rate begins to rise and there is no guarantee of a consistent mortgage payment. If you only intend to stay in the home for a short period of time (preferably the fixed-rate period) or you have no problem refinancing, this might be a great option for you since you will pay less interest to the bank.

Bill's family's first home was a foreclosure back in the late '80s, while his second home was an FHA purchase of an estate sale. He moved into the second home with built-in equity, though at the time, travel and entertainment was far more important than saving and investing in the future, hence the reason for having to use an instrument with a low down payment requirement. Taking advantage of the FHA loan program is a great way for first-time buyers, or anyone with a shortage of down payment funds, to buy a home. Additionally, FHA financing allows for the financing of manufactured homes on a permanent foundation, as many lenders do not finance these properties. With current land values, this is a great alternative for first-time homebuyers in areas with expensive land. Yes, these properties do also get foreclosed on. As long as it is taxed as real estate, and the bank has not been paid, the property can be purchased at a significant savings to the actual market or appraised value.

However, you should be aware that the FHA does not make home loans. According to homebuying.about.com, if a buyer defaults, the lender is paid from the insurance fund. To get an FHA loan, you must have good credit history and sufficient income to qualify, because like other insurance policies the organization does not want you to have to use it! FHA loans require that your monthly housing costs not exceed 29 percent of your gross (before tax) monthly income. Total housing costs includes your mortgage principle, interest, property taxes, and insurance. Those four items are referred to as PITI. Homebuying.about.com uses the following formula to help you determine the maximum monthly payment you can qualify for:

Monthly income x .29 = Maximum PITI

In their example, a monthly income of $3,000 gross means that you qualify for $3,000 multiplied by .29, for an $870 maximum PITI. Note that this assumes you are paying down principle. You can easily see here why it is so important to look at other loan options.

Another requirement is that long-term debt plus PITI can be no more than 41 percent of your gross monthly income. This includes credit cards and auto loans. In their example to calculate total income qualification:

Monthly income x .41 = Maximum Total Monthly Costs

For the same $3,000 monthly income, all of your long-term expenses cannot exceed $1,230 ($3,000 multiplied by .41). This is not to say that

FHA will not allow you to have a higher front-end PITI ratio if, for example, you do not have other consumer debt but still remain within the .41 ratio they like to see. Additionally, in some of the higher value states, FHA loans may go to 50 percent total debt, with certain compensating factors. These are great programs for a first time homebuyer who purchases a foreclosure. Investors should know, however, that FHA does not underwrite investment properties or second homes. It stands to reason that the government does not want to guarantee anything other than a primary residence when there is only a 3 percent contribution on the side of the buyer.

Also note that non-FHA loans will usually let you go even higher on the total debt ratios, and are based on the payment amount, which is one of the reasons many negative amortization (NegAm) owners have been getting into trouble—they easily qualify while they aren't even covering their interest, but once they have to, they cannot pay. $1,230 minus the PITI of $870 means that other monthly long-term debt (which does not include utilities, by the way) cannot exceed $360. Additionally, non-FHA loans can be used for non-owner occupied homes, such as investment properties and second homes.

Remember that FICO discussion mentioned earlier in the book? Well, once again, it is an important factor in determining the allowable debt-to-income ratio. This of course will also impact your ability to purchase a foreclosure property, particularly if the subject property is an REO or BPO. The owning bank does not want to see the house come back as a foreclosure in the future. Often for a standard conventional home loan, PITI cannot exceed 26 to 28 percent of gross monthly income, and 33 to 36 percent of total expenses. This is the absolutely most conservative threshold used in lending.

In higher-cost states, it is permissible to have higher debt-to-income ratios. If they did not exist, most people in these high-cost areas would not be able to afford homes based on the specified criteria. During the intense housing crunch when lenders were finding creative ways to finance just about everyone, these same ratios (or higher depending on your credit score) were applied to interest-only or negative amortization payments, hence the recent laws in some states requiring that the borrower qualify not only for the interest only payment, but for the payment once it is fully indexed or fully amortized.

Check out www.RealtyTrac.com/news/ press/FinancialCalculators.asp to see various tools pertaining to rent versus buy, home affordability, loan consolidation, and mortgage qualification.

If you want to obtain an FHA loan, you have to have the credit to show you meet your monthly obligations; in other words, it must be in good shape. This does not mean credit needs to be perfect. FHA is pretty forgiving, but you must make enough money, as noted above. You must have enough cash available to make the 3 percent down payment at the time of closing, and you must be able to pay closing costs, which are roughly two to three percent of the price of the home (often including homeowners insurance prepaid, attorney's fees where required, title search, title insurance, PMI if required, loan origination fees, and a fee that goes into the FHA insurance fund, which individuals not using an FHA loan do not have to pay). In addition, you may have to pay points to the lender. Some people do this to "buy down" a prepayment penalty. Others do this to buy down interest rates, and others are assessed points due to less-than-stellar credit.

Veterans Administration (VA) Loans

Just like FHA, the Veterans Administration insures loans but does not fund them. These are loans for individuals who have served a qualified military service and often are easier to qualify for with less stringent down payments when purchasing over the conforming loan limits, or no down payment at all if within the conforming loan limits (Metrocities). Some organizations believe that VA home loans are the best benefit a veteran gets. According to vamortgagecenter.com, almost every veteran is eligible for VA benefits including VA loans, and they are good for both purchasing homes and refinancing existing mortgages. If you are a veteran wanting to buy a foreclosure, get a copy of your honorable discharge, or DD-214 Certificate of Eligibility, or your active duty confirmation through the VA office.

What are some of the ways you qualify? If you served (as defined by the VA) during wartime for at least 90 consecutive days or peacetime for at least 181 consecutive days, you are eligible for the VA Home Loan program. If you are currently on active duty after 90 days of active service, you are also eligible for the program. Reservists are also eligible if they have served at least six years, and qualified Reserve branches include the Army National Guard, Army Reserve, Air National Guard, Coast Guard Reserve, Navy Reserve, Marine Corps Reserve, and the Air Force Reserve. There are others eligible too, including spouses of veterans who died as a result of their active service or a service-related injury (as long as they are not remarried), of soldiers missing in action, or of prisoners of war that are members of the Armed Forces and have been missing for over 90 days. U.S. citizens who served with an allied country during World War II also may be eligible, something veterans often aren't aware of.

Currently, the maximum entitlement a veteran receives is $36,000 but this can be up to $60,000 for loans that exceed $144,000. This does not mean your maximum loan can be $144,000—in fact as of the date of writing this the maximum loan is $417,000. The $144,000 refers to the amount the VA guarantees to the bank. By guaranteeing your loan to a bank, the VA alleviates mortgage insurance known as Principle Mortgage Insurance (PMI) that is often applied if your loan-to-value ratio is over 80 percent.

Since there is no time limit to use your benefits, you can use them anytime. You can buy a home with no down payment and low interest rates. Another great feature that most people do not know about? If you use your entitlement and then pay the loan by getting a new loan, refinancing, or buying another house, you can use your entitlement again because you already repaid the guarantees. This is not true, however, if you simply transfer your loan to someone else because the entitlements are still outstanding (vamortgagecenter.com).

Last but certainly not least, a VA loan is an excellent way to help reestablish credit for those individuals who were honorably discharged but along the way ignored some financial obligations or were unaware of the ability to defer payments while on military duty. Remember that as long as you qualify based on income, a VA loan does not consider credit history under most circumstances. Credit scores that would typically mean a significant down payment or subprime interest rates can still work under VA guidelines. If you are looking to purchase a foreclosure home with a VA loan, you will need to live in the home as an owner occupied residence. VA will not underwrite for investment properties.

No-Documentation and Low-Documentation Loans

Lots of investors use these types of loans. A "no-doc" loan is simply more convenient for people who do not want to go through the income verification process. Individuals who are self-employed usually need this type of loan as their income perhaps isn't verifiable, or their write-offs are so extreme that the net income they report does not allow them to qualify.

We both can verify our income trails but because of their sheer complexity, we choose not to. We'd rather spend our time working to educate our readers and clients about the real estate market than spend time collecting materials for a mortgage. The cost isn't much different for our loan types anyway, particularly when the time we spend gathering the information can be better spent on investing and researching trends before they really happen.

Understandably, mortgages are made based on the presumption of risk based on several factors that we will discuss in various sections of this book. An understanding of these risks is important, as it is the foundation for your ability to purchase primary homes and eventually foreclosures. Years ago, before Bill worked with investors on a frequent basis, he had the following learning experience. A self-employed borrower confirmed that they reported over $3 million in income per year, which was used to qualify them for the mortgage. Since they had several exotic vehicles and fit the economic profile, there was little reason to doubt their information. As the lending institution underwent document preparation, tax returns confirmed their gross income as reported, only to show a total of $32,000 in net income—yes, all of the rest was written off. While this type of situation does not mean that the borrower cannot qualify, it certainly means that they cannot prove their income based on their complete tax returns. To the lender, they have no reason to extend the lowest qualifying rate in the absence of sufficient documentation to mitigate the risk.

People with less than perfect credit, only a little bit of credit or no type of credit also often go for this loan type as well (Metrocities). The requirements for these loan types, however, are beginning to increase. Recently, major lenders, particularly in the subprime area, have made major announcements that they are re-purchasing billions of dollars in loans that had an early payment default as a result of declining values and overly liberal underwriting guidelines. This has essentially assured that the flow of homes in foreclosure will be plentiful to say the least. Many of these loans were no-doc loans, particularly for buyers with a poor credit history, combined with a lack of assets that were not properly verified. Although not huge, there is a penalty in the interest rate of a no-doc loan and there are fewer lenders providing this type of loan.

There are similar programs, referred to as low-doc loans, that people with good credit may qualify for. This type of loan requires some but not much documentation. Interestingly enough, individuals sometimes choose to use this loan type to protect their privacy, though we're not entirely convinced it achieves that goal. Bear in mind that if your goal is to purchase one foreclosure as an investment, or what will become a portfolio of foreclosures, you will need to put your best foot forward from the start. Specifically, a mortgage banker or consultant that is not used to working with investors will only collect enough information to make that individual deal work.

Dani recently encountered a lender that didn't understand how to work with investors. The lender wanted documentation on every rental property to tie every rental with her credit report, and to see leases for each property. The lender also wanted documentation of income, which due to the nature of her job, changes drastically month to month. The lender unknowingly was setting Dani up for future issues with loans because income would change (even though it is all legitimate change) and the lender has previous records. It is imperative that any and all assets are properly disclosed from the beginning, as the same lender will certainly question your new-found income and/or assets if they do not pass a test of reasonability when you come back for additional mortgages. As with any other professional relationship—medical, legal, financial, or others—disclosure is paramount for us to adequately and appropriately serve your needs. All too often it is believed that the goal is to push the borrower into a higher interest rate; this is certainly not the case with the majority of professionals in the business who depend completely on referral business as a result of their stellar reputation.

In a no-doc loan, the borrower isn't presenting lots of documentation to qualify. Usually, you will have to show proof of employment *history* (different than currently employed), financial documentation, and credit history. If you have a high credit score, you may also choose not to divulge any specific financial or employment records and in exchange for this privacy, you will pay a higher interest rate. Home loan applicants who gain income from "under the table" resources, are self employed, live off of commission only and do not have a standard paycheck, or who work part time or on a contract basis had no way to fund loans in the past. Today, these types of individuals can go the no-doc route (presuming they have a decent credit history).

Another option is a no-ratio home loan, which requires only some asset information along with a lender credit report (you cannot go to mycreditscore.com and give it to the bank) and an appraisal.

With both loan types, there are three main categories of loans.

1. *The no-ratio loan* in which the lender does not require any particular debt-to-income ratio information normally standard for other loan types. In fact, this type does not even require the borrower to state his or her income; if someone is living solely on investments or has an unsure financial situation, this may be a good option. Asset verification is critical for this type of loan. Be prepared to pay in the price though, as well as in the maximum loan to value, and

loan amount. The less information a borrower can or will provide, the greater the level of risk.

2. *The no income/no asset (NINA) loan* requires some documentation including name, social security number, and the address of the property the borrower is purchasing. The lender does check credit and completes an appraisal. This sort of loan typically works for middle- to higher-income individuals with complicated investments, including but not limited to overseas deposits or income streams.

3. *The stated income loan* is a loan that requires you to state your income without verification of income statements, W2s, or tax returns, but should be looking at cash flow from bank statements during a three-month to twelve-month period. This is a good choice if your income includes cash, tips, gifts, etc., and where stated income for tax purposes isn't necessarily valid. This is great for self-employed individuals or people who primarily live off their investments (Mortgage News Daily). This type of program also works for salaried workers such as mechanics, architects, plumbers, or other professional or service personnel that have the ability to moonlight for additional income.

So what's the penalty for all of this good news? The rates for these mortgages, depending on credit and how much information you are willing to supply, are usually .5 to 3 percent higher than a conventional loan.

The other thing to remember with these programs is that for just about any income level and credit profile, there is a mortgage to help you get started investing in foreclosures. This does not mean that you can have a history of late payments, or make minimum wage with no savings, but you'll be pleased to see that getting started simply requires a lot of research and preparation. This book should be a great start for you to get started. By having picked up this book, you have a step-by-step manual to begin building a real estate portfolio.

Negative Amortization Mortgages (NegAm)

This negative amortization mortgage has gotten a lot of bad press lately, not all undeserved. This type of mortgage has been an incredible lifesaver for a lot of people. It has allowed lots of individuals to buy homes that they otherwise may not have been able to afford, and use the money they're saving on mortgage payments to pay down high-interest debt, invest in other properties, or even buy foreclosures! These types of loans also make it easy for investment properties to generate a "cash flow," or make money on a monthly basis (rent paid to the homeowner minus the mortgage payment, taxes, and insurance). They have allowed people who know they'll be earning more in the future, expect large performance bonuses, or who feel very confident that their home will increase in equity appreciation to buy a home or live in an area they may not have otherwise been able to previously consider. But they are also contributing to the number of defaults. Let us explain more.

Negative amortization mortgages ADD to your balance each month. Contrary to any claims to the opposite, the lowest payment option ALWAYS defers interest and almost always accumulates interest to the balance at a higher rate than if you were paying the interest.

NegAm loans are perfectly suited for people who truly understand them. Like other mortgages, they can be financial management tools that offer a high level of flexibility to those who understand the benefits as well as the risks. Lots of mortgage brokers and even lenders are paid greater commissions if the home buyer chooses this type of loan, so you must understand why the mortgage companies choose to do this before committing. Simply put, it is an extremely profitable product. Lenders are charging higher interest rates for the "option" to accumulate more debt. We'll explain more about that shortly. In addition, tax and income rules allow the lender to claim the entire payment that *would have been made* as revenue, even though it is just added to the balance of the loan.

There are obviously many benefits for the lender, and the borrower has many too. In fact, this type of loan has been so popular that a full 25 percent of loans are of this nature. There are zip codes in the U.S. where, in 2005, 100 percent of loans were purchased or refinanced using negative amortization loans. One particular zip code had properties valued in the multi-million dollar range, so one has to infer that the individuals or families that live there know how to utilize this type of mortgage as a tool.

The NegAm mortgage allows the borrower the option each month to make payments that are less *than the interest that accrues on the loan.* Immediately, you can imagine the benefits and drawbacks. This means that if the borrower only pays the lowest monthly option (often referred to as a Pay Option ARM, or a Pick-a-Payment Loan because of this opportunity) the loan balance will *increase* by the amount of interest not paid. The loan is structured as a four-tiered loan on a 30- or 40-year option with a negative amortization, or deferred interest option, as the primary attraction. The additional payment options are interest-only based on a 30-year amortization, a 30-year fixed, and a 15-year fixed, all of which are subject to a set index and a margin that depends on credit quality and overall loan to value. For example, according to year-end 2006, information on www.census.gov, the price point with the highest amount of sales units on the west coast was the $300,000 to $499,999 range.

Using an average in the range of $400,000, Bill created a sample loan payment with current indices and margins. With this type of program, the lowest payment option with these parameters would be $1,287 per month, not including taxes and insurance. The interest-only option for the first month would be $2,480 based on the fully indexed rate. Simply put, the difference between the two payment options is the amount of interest that is deferred, or simply added to the balance. In this case, $1,193 is added to the balance the first month, or a minimum of $14,316 in deferred interest the first year.

What is the advantage? Presumably if the rate of appreciation on the home is greater than this deferred interest amount, then the program served its purpose. Also, if you purchase a foreclosure property at a significant discount, this program will help your monthly cash flow while you watch the property appreciate back to its normal standing in the marketplace. The interest rate is higher, of course, on the negative amortization loan, so more is getting added to the balance than would have been paid if the borrower was paying on an interest-only loan. You have to decide if you really need the ability to pay a low amount; if you do, this is a good loan option.

Recent changes in the NegAm program allow for this amount to be fixed for a period of time, namely a five-year period during which the deferred interest amount is locked. With the current programs however, the rate tends to adjust every month. While ever so slight, one comes to realize that the other three payment options continue to rise each month, which causes a higher monthly payment to stay current, or a larger deferment of interest.

While these loans do carry a greater risk for the bank, they also usually result in a higher interest payment, which means that interest the borrower accrues does so at a faster rate than most other types of mortgages. Even if the owner goes into bankruptcy, the bank earns more money. On the example noted above, the market interest rate on a 30-year fixed-rate loan is 6.375, while the same rate option on the Option Arm is 7.458—more than a whole point higher. Now, one can imagine that if this subject property is worth $600,000, and there exists $200,000 worth of equity; all factors being equal, a minimum of $14,316 of interest will be added to that balance, effectively chipping into the equity.

As we have discussed, this program can be used successfully as an investment and cash-flow tool. We do not recommend it, however, to anyone without a significant equity position, strong financial discipline, or at the very least a strong understanding of the program. If, as a consumer, you will be paying at least the interest amount on a consistent basis, you should opt for an interest-only loan or ARM. This type of program is an ideal situation for someone who does not have regular steady income, or has very complicated finances. With the guidance of an experienced financial planner or Certified Public Accountant, this person can utilize this type of program. We absolutely caution that if you need to pay the minimum to afford the payment, you need to be very, very careful, or at the very least have a significant down payment of 20 percent or greater. A first-time homebuyer who is unable to verify income and has a low credit score should stay away from this program, statistics expect that home will go into foreclosure. Conversely, if you have excellent credit with a score over 750, you may qualify for this type of program with no money down if you can show you have twelve months of reserves in the bank to cover the expected payments for a full year.

It is important to know that NegAm mortgages have a loan-to-value cap that can eventually devastate a homeowner, so read onto the next section.

NegAm Mortgages and Increasing Defaults

After looking through the types of mortgages, it is easy to see why people with NegAm mortgages may be more likely to default. These are very complicated financial instruments; individuals must look beyond the low monthly payment, which many lenders fail to appropriately disclose.

But there is an additional caveat we have not yet mentioned. Most NegAm mortgages have a loan-to-value cap. This means that the loan to value (the principle amount owed) can never exceed a percent of its original amount. Let's assume you borrow $1 million on a $1.2 million home, using a NegAm mortgage. Let's assume also that the loan has a 125 percent max cap—meaning that once the accruing interest creates a balance of $1,250,000, the loan will fully amortize and you will owe the full principle and interest payment, due within the remaining years of the loan. An individual with a $2,800 per month NegAm payment that has been paying the minimum may suddenly find themselves with a $6,000 or more monthly payment, at a higher interest rate than an interest-only or a fixed-rate mortgage. This is a shock for most people, and often causes default. If the home does not have enough equity to refinance, the homeowner may be stuck paying this large payment or going into foreclosure.

Banks were allowing homeowners to go to 125 percent on their mortgages, but many are pulling back due to excess risk and only allowing 110 percent now. As banks tightened the credit standards for lending, they began to loosen the standards slightly by pushing the cap back up to 115 percent. This occurs as a balancing act to keep supply and demand in check. After all, the banks are mostly publicly traded companies, meaning they must continue to lend money taking some level of risk. This means that depending on the maximum caps and thresholds, you could very quickly hit your cap and have a fully amortized payment to deal with.

Look at the lenders that have originated these loans so aggressively, and you will find a high amount of foreclosure activity, particularly loans that were originated in 2004 and 2005 respectively (First American, 2006). So again, if you are looking to purchase a property for yourself, or an investment property, you can be certain that the mortgage companies that originated all of these loans will be the same ones who will be managing their rapidly growing books of foreclosure properties.

Another major caveat? Many people get themselves out of financial jams, at least temporarily, by taking out second mortgages or equity lines on their homes. But many banks do not want to take the risk of being in a "subordinate position" (second) behind a NegAm first mortgage. In the case of default, the primary lien holder gets paid first, and then the secondary lien holder. If you owe more on your first mortgage than your home is worth, the second lien holder stands in a position to possibly get nothing from the auction sale or REO sale of the home. By the way, Bill has seen homes that have third, fourth, and even fifth positions for those individuals who own their own businesses, have SBA loans, or paid a significant sum to these higher risk loans.

If the bank does loan you money on a home with a NegAm first, they assume that the loan is maxed out (in our example, they assume you owe $1,250,000) and then they assume you have no equity to lend against, since the home is only worth $1,200,000. The only option is to pay down the loan enough that it can be refinanced.

The NegAm is a great option if you want flexibility and you can pay the full payment if you need to. It is also a great option if you intend to sell the home fairly quickly (though watch for steep pre-payment penalties). This brings us to another point that is very important to discuss and become aware of when shopping for a mortgage. Before we move to prepayment penalties, however, let's touch on one other creative mortgage.

Reverse Mortgage

Borrowers often confuse reverse mortgages and negative amortization mortgages and inaccurately use the terms interchangeably, so we will discuss them briefly. A reverse mortgage is a loan against your home that you *do not have to pay back as long as you are living in it.* You can borrow up to 65 percent of the home's appraised value, but there are a lot of restrictions. You must be at least 62 years of age, and you must have enough equity in the home to meet the 65 percent rule. There are no income or credit requirements, but you must occupy this home as your primary residence (Metrocities). Unless the foreclosure you are buying is your retirement home, you will most likely not be looking at this type of loan for your purchase. Additionally, the fees on these mortgages typically average a minimum of two points, which makes them very expensive.

> Many officials are crying foul when it comes to negative amortization mortgages, which they blame for the increase in foreclosure properties. In California, foreclosures were up 76 percent in Los Angeles in November 2006 alone, and over 115 percent during Quarter 4 2005 to Quarter 4 2006. Even in the wealthier Orange County, the same month had an increase of 33 percent in foreclosure rates. California had 19,248 filings in that same one-month period, an increase of 20 percent over the previous month.

Prepayment Penalties

There are two types of prepayment penalties, which is essentially where the bank charges you money for paying off your loan early. One should understand that lenders look at prepayment penalties beyond one year as an incentive to the mortgage originators who bring these loans to them; there is rarely a time that the penalty is necessary. Lenders want you to continue paying interest and this is a way to deter you from not doing that.

A hard penalty is by far the worst; this is where the loan cannot be refinanced or even sold without a penalty during the prepay time period. Usually this prepayment period is one year, but it can vary from one to three or more, so be sure to check. A soft prepay means that you can sell the home without penalty but you can't refinance. The less interest the bank collects from you (such as the case with NegAm mortgages), the greater the prepayment penalty will be because they want to guarantee they will at least get a certain amount of profit from you before you refinance or sell. If you know you have a great rate, feel confident you will not need to refinance, and you like your bank, you may want to ask for a higher term prepay to lower the interest rate. Some banks will do this.

Conversely, you should clarify that your loan does not carry a prepayment penalty beyond one year, if at all. Certain companies do not use prepayment penalties at all, while other major lenders, whom we will not name, provide incentives as a percentage of the loan amount in exchange for a long prepayment penalty. A recent scenario with a major lender had the company offering a one time $750 incentive to the originator in exchange for a prepayment penalty that charged a 3 percent prepayment fee of the original loan amount. In the specific scenario, a $500,000 loan would generate a $15,000 prepayment penalty to the bank—$750 in incentive money was a great deal! The disclosure for this should be clear in the Truth In Lending statement in most mortgage documents.

Finding the facts

Prepayment penalties over one year are generally unnecessary, except in extreme credit situations. Review any documents to ensure you understand the length of time you are committing to keeping a loan.

Additionally, unscrupulous lenders and brokers will have a mortgage addendum that adds the prepayment fee to the loan. Be vigilant about checking for prepayment penalties. If you are scheduled to close an escrow within a few days and this fee is a surprise or not appropriately disclosed, ensure that the documents are re-drawn without the fee or you can expect to pay a significant amount of money down the line. Do not succumb to the fear that you are going to lose the home and allow this to occur. The real estate agents and any other interested parties should be immediately notified.

Owner-Occupied and Nonowner-Occupied (NOO) Residencies

When you apply for a mortgage, you will be asked if this will be your primary residence. If you already have a primary residence and you say yes, you will need to explain this by either showing your home is on the market or getting a notarized letter stating that your new home will be for primary residencial purposes, that your existing home is or will be rented out (and provide a copy of the lease), and/or that documents your existing home's for-sale status. Additionally, that test of reasonableness comes back up again. For example, say you live in a 4,000 square foot home near the beach. You decide to purchase a duplex in which each unit is 850 square feet, and you intend to live in one of the units. Convince the lender of the logic of your plan to reduce your living space by over 75 percent, and that lender will go to bat for you in underwriting—in most cases. These clarifications are necessary for the underwriter to make the loan resalable on the secondary market.

Owner-occupied residencies means that you will live there. If you are buying a foreclosure to live in it, then your loan is an owner-occupied loan. If you are not intending to live in it and want to use it as a rental, it is nonowner occupied. The exception to the primary residence requirement is that most banks allow second homes (vacation homes), so if you intend to use it as such, say so. This will generally keep your interest rate at the same level as an owner-occupied loan. Again, logic prevails that the second home should be in a vacation or resort destination, or even a distance of one hundred miles or greater from your primary residence, where it would make sense as a "getaway" residence. Let's make it clear; an owner-occupied residence will get better rates and be a better overall package than a nonowner-occupied residence, as there is a presumption of care on the part of the owner. Banks know it is harder for a person calling a house a home to leave it than it is for someone to abandon a house that has a tenant living in it or is vacant. Better rates mean lower down payments, better interest rates, lower or no pre-payment penalties, and other more favorable lending positions.

This does not mean you shouldn't buy foreclosures for investment purposes, only that you cannot simply compare the rates you see on eloan.com to what your lender gives you for a NOO house. Attempting to do this is like comparing the taste of an apple to that of an orange. Before you think of trying to convince the lender that you'll be buying a foreclosure in the same town that you live in, but it will be a second home, just realize that most lenders and underwriters can see right through the story. You can, however, compare the quote the lender gives you, discussed in the Good Faith Estimate portion below, with what other lenders give you for the same situation.

Good Faith Estimate (GFE)

When you go through the process of acquiring a home loan for any purpose including purchasing foreclosures, the bank will give you a good faith estimate. This is a written estimate of the estimated costs of doing business, including the lender's fees and the agents' charges and fees. It will include estimated costs for taxes and insurance too. All lenders must present a good faith estimate to clients.

This GFE will let you make a more informed decision and will help you compare banks, too. However, a word to the wise: The mortgage industry is rife with companies and individuals who fail to properly disclose a true accounting of the estimate of charges because they "low-ball" the costs necessary to close a mortgage loan. If you have allowed the individual handling your financing to review your credit, and have discussed your options, you should receive an extremely accurate Good Faith Estimate as required by law.

GFE Guarantee

Many companies will offer a guarantee of their own fees. Bill is aware of one company that issued a guarantee of all non-recurring closing costs, including the title, escrow (or attorney in certain states) charges that are passed on to the customer. That company is Cambridge Funding Group located in Laguna Hills, California. The President of the company, Bill

Butler, has been in the mortgage business for over 30 years. He is a consummate professional and believes this practice will create a competitive advantage moving forward. Additionally, the Western Mortgage Group has a strategic relationship with Prudential California Realty, operated by another team of well-respected real estate professionals, Rich and Annette Cosner, who have been in the real estate business since 1972 and 1984 respectively. Keep an eye out for these types of operations as you they are poised for growth in the coming years. Bill was so impressed with Prudential California Realty that he went to work for the company.

What's in the GFE?

According to *Mortgage Daily News*,

> The good faith estimate is divided into sections of similar fees, each of which is designated by a range of numbers: the 800s, 900s, 1000s, 1100s, 1200s, and 1300s. For purposes of comparison-shopping, the most significant fees are listed in the 800s. Most of the items are within the control of the lender or broker, so the estimates should be accurate. A few of the items in the 800s are charged by third parties, however, and the lender's estimates should not be far off from the actual charges. The lender has direct control over origination and discount points and fees (listed in 801 and 802) and administrative, underwriting, processing, funding, document preparation, wire transfer, and other fees (listed in 810 and higher).

Third party fees contained in the 800s are usually appraisals, the credit report, inspection, mortgage insurance, assumption, tax service, and flood certifications. These fees are supposed to be passed on to you, the borrower, with no added markups or fees. Some national lenders own subsidiaries to provide these services so the estimates are accurate. We always recommend padding up to 5 percent (or 105 percent of the overall GFE amount) to cover yourself and to make sound decisions. As a buyer, this will be wise until a greater number of mortgage companies more aggressively guarantee the costs that they, as well as third party operators, charge to the customer. A recent analysis of an estimated closing statement showed over $7,000 worth of junk fees by the escrow and title companies. According to *Mortgage News Daily*,

> Fees denoted in the 1300 series (surveys and pest inspections) should also be easy for lenders to estimate accurately. The 900s and 1000s concern prepaid items, such as mortgage, hazard and flood insurance premiums, mortgage interest and taxes that must be paid up front or deposited into an escrow account. The 1100s cover title charges, title insurance premiums, settlement or escrow fees, and attorney and notary charges. Items contained in the 1200 consist of government fees such as city and county tax stamps and recording fees. Charges contained in the 900 to 1200 series are difficult to estimate. Some of the prepaid amounts vary based on the date of closing. For example, the borrower would have to prepay a full month's interest if he or she closed on the first of the month, but not if he or she closed on the last.

Author's Notes

Dani once gave three lenders one lender's GFE, and asked them all to beat it. One lender happens to be the co-author of this book. He was able to beat the other's GFEs and ultimately won the business on a large purchase over a lender she'd worked with for years. Do not be afraid to share GFEs with lenders; in fact, use them as a bargaining tool!

Demand Clarification

GFEs are often difficult to read and understand. As mentioned earlier, ask your finance company, lender, or broker, whatever questions you need in order to be an informed consumer. Don't fall victim to being rushed into signing documents that do not come close to the original good faith estimate that is provided. You are typically working with a 30-day window from origination to closing; it should not be difficult to expect an accurate estimate of closing costs that gets you in the ballpark of costs.

Rate Locks

If you have a bank giving you a great interest rate, ask for a rate lock. You can do this once you have identified a property and can commit a lock that is often good for 30 to 45 days. While you may also request a lock as short as 15 days, you may commit to a longer lock period of 60 or 90 days and sometimes even longer. It all depends on the property you are buying, whether the courts are involved, or if there are any potential delays. Remember that the longer you lock, you are committing funds that become speculative for you and the bank, and their risk, as well as the capital markets, will be reflected in the price you pay for the protection. Additionally, you may choose not to lock your rate, referred to as "floating." This will allow you to benefit from the markets when rates are generally on the downswing, but also expose you to added risk if the markets or rates are volatile, and rates are increasing.

Communicate with your lender to make sure they are not exposing you to unnecessary risk by floating your rate without your authorization, and attempting to lock the rate so they can capture sales. Find out if the lender will let you unlock if the rate drops. While it may be good to speculate the market, it may also carry risks that the market turns negatively on you; do not ask your lender what he or she thinks the rates will do unless he or she is a friend and will not make any money off of your rate. Watch the market; watch business shows with experts—anything you can do to have an educated guess as to how interest rates are expected to perform in the next 30 to 60 days so you are aware of what you are locking.

Credit Score

Another major element that will impact the type of loan you qualify for and the interest rate you pay is your credit score. This may be one of the most important items to look at. Since subprime mortgages tend to go into foreclosure in an average of less than two years, or often even months, your bank needs to know your credit worthiness. Subprime mortgages are commonly associated with borrowers with poor or marginal credit, though certain unsavory lenders and brokers will place less sophisticated borrowers with great credit into these mortgages unknowingly.

Since we advise you to pre-qualify for a loan before making an offer to a distressed homeowner or in an auction (which will require it anyway), you need to know what your credit score is. There are lots of expert books on credit and how to boost your score, so we'll focus on what you need for lending purposes. Credit score can drastically impact your interest rates. If you have a FICO score of 720, you may be paying a full three or more percentage points less in interest than someone with a 580. On a $100,000 loan (who can buy a house these days for that?) that is an additional $2,400 per year, assuming a 5.5 and 8.5 percent rate, respectively.

FICO is a score determined by the Fair Isaac Corporation and is the most commonly used credit scoring system. Scores range from 300 to 850, and most people score in the 600s to 700s. Lenders can buy your score from three credit reporting agencies, also called bureaus. These three companies are Experian, Equifax, and TransUnion. You also have the ability to view your own credit report online once per year at www.annualcreditreport.com, where you will have free access to one report from each bureau per year. You will need to pay between $5 to $8 for your score, but will not need to sign up for complimentary monitoring or the host of other items that are offered by most bureaus.

Finding the facts

Increased credit score requirements by lenders and banks are designed to prevent future loan defaults from occurring. Unfortunately, they create a negative impact on borrowers with credit scores below 700. The U.S. median is approximately 723. The best rates are given to those with scores about 770.

Bear in mind that most lenders consider a credit score above 720 as being strong, 681 to 719 as being above average, 640 to 680 as being average, and anything below that being slightly below average until you dip below 620 which places you as high risk to lenders which may have an interest penalty or result in a decline of credit altogether. Each agency does calculate your score differently, resulting in a credit score that can change on a daily basis. Remember that credit scoring is a snapshot of your credit performance at the time it is pulled. It is not uncommon to see significant swings in credit scoring. Knowing this, lenders will pull the score from all three bureaus and typically use the middle score.

What is Reflected in Your Credit Score?

Your payment history is about 35 percent of your score. This includes paying bills on time and not having any bankruptcies or late payments.

Solid payment history helps your score. If, for some reason, you have a late payment, referred to as a delinquency, the newer the default, the worse the impact will be on your score. A recent borrower was adamant that her score was in the 790 to 810 range, which would have placed this borrower in the top 1 percent of credit scoring nationwide, only to find two medical collection accounts with an aggregate debt of under $200 that caused her score to drop to 665. It may seem immaterial, but it made a significant impact on her rates for the first and second mortgages. Also, people say "but I've never been late!" when they have an average or poor score. This is because history is only a little more than a third of the calculation. You'll see why this occurs as we continue this discussion.

Another third of your score is based on how much you owe, or what is called credit utilization. This includes all accounts and their balances, along with how much of their available credit they are using. This is one of many reasons we recommend keeping your balances down (especially on credit cards or lines of credit that let you go over your available credit). The more you owe compared to your credit limit, the greater the negative impact on your score. Also, it is important to know that your credit grantor correctly reports your available limit to the bureaus, otherwise the bureau will assume that your balance is at its limit. A certain credit card issuer that often wonders, "What is in your wallet?" is notorious for not reporting credit limits.

The length of your credit history only accounts for about 15 percent of the score. Longer credit histories increase scores but you can have a high number with a short credit history if you have used your credit responsibly. There are lots of ways to build credit, including secured credit cards and car loans that you pay promptly and even pay off ahead of schedule. This is not to say that you should rush out and open multiple credit accounts, believing that you will have a high score from the start. Again, there is a mathematical formula that looks at various factors when generating a credit score.

New credit accounts for about 10 percent of your score. This is commonly referred to as inquiries. If you open new credit accounts, this will affect your score. Resist the temptation to get 10 percent off at your favorite department store by opening a card. Most reporting agencies do note whether you were opening a credit card or searching for a loan through many new credit lines based on the length of time over which the inquiries occur. If you are loan searching, do your rate shopping within a very specific period of time, preferably within a 10- to 14-day window, as credit scoring is designed to not penalize you for mortgage shopping during this tight timeframe. If you decide to include purchasing a vehicle and opening other consumer credit in a short span of time, expect to pay for it in your credit score. Also, these inquiries should result in at least one line of extended credit.

Finally, other miscellaneous factors make up the other 10 percent or so of your score. Having a mix of credit card types on your credit report, installment loans such as mortgages and lines of credit, multiple mortgage and auto loans, and personal lines of credit are all normal for people with longer credit histories and can boost your score slightly.

All of the data mentioned above is part of the Fair Isaac Corporation's FICO model. There is also a new scoring system that has been developed as a joint agreement with Experian, Equifax, and TransUnion; the model, called VantageScore, may be used in the future.

Marital status, race, color, religion, national origin, dependence or receipt of money from public assistance, and gender cannot affect your credit score under the federal Equal Credit Opportunity Act or the Fair Credit Reporting Act.

If you do not want to use an online company to get your credit report, there are other options. See the table on the opposite page from the Federal Citizen Information Center for some options.

Prime and Subprime Lending

Prime and subprime lending are terms we hear often, yet they are nearly as often misunderstood. Prime lenders are those who offer loans to individuals with near perfect credit and offer the best rates because they take on the lowest risk. For those who have some credit problems or want

Recommended Sources for Credit Scores

Source	Cost	Description	Score Range
ANNUAL CREDIT REPORT SERVICE Congress established this outlet to make it easier for consumers to get their credit reports and credit scores from the three national credit-reporting agencies. **Web:**www.annualcreditreport.com **Phone:** 1-877-322-8228 **U.S. Mail:** Annual Credit Report Request Service P. O. Box 105281 Atlanta, GA 30348-5281	The price for credit scores is being determined by the Federal Trade Commission. One free credit report per year from each credit-reporting agency.	Each credit-reporting agency offers a different type of credit score to consumers.	FICO score via: Equifax 300-850 Experian 330-830 TransUnion 150-934
MYFICO.COM The consumer internet site of Fair Isaac Corporation that developed the FICO score. **Web:** www.myfico.com	$14.95 for one FICO score and credit report. $44.85 for all three FICO scores and credit reports from the three credit reporting agencies (2006 pricing).	This score is most often used by lenders. It lets you see how prospective lenders would evaluate your credit history.	FICO score from Equifax, Experian, and/or Trans Union 300-850
INDIVIDUAL CREDIT REPORTING AGENCIES: **EQUIFAX** **Web:** www.equifax.com **Phone:** 1-800-685-1111 **EXPERIAN** **Web:** www.experian.com **Phone:** 1 866 200 6020 **TRANSUNION** **Web:** www.transunion.com **Phone:** 1-800-888-4213	Prices for credit scores with credit reports vary from $14.95 to $34.95 (2006 pricing).	Each credit-reporting agency offers a different type of credit score to consumers.	FICO score via Equifax 300-850 Experian 330-830 TransUnion 150-934
MORTGAGE LENDERS	Credit score is free when applying for mortgage or home equity loan.	This score will likely be the actual score used to evaluate your application. Ask your lender to be sure.	FICO score from Equifax, Experian, or Trans Union 300-850

Information from www.pueblo.gsa.gov/cic_text/money/creditscores/your.htm

flexible loan terms, subprime lending is another option. By no means does this mean that creditworthy individuals cannot be placed into subprime mortgages. Often referred to as predatory lending, several minority individuals who are completely creditworthy are placed into higher interest rate and higher fee programs when it was absolutely unnecessary to do so. Inform yourself as a consumer, assuring you have a copy of your credit report and appropriate disclosure early on in the transaction. The person running your credit check should have no issue whatsoever in providing you with your credit report. If for some reason they do not wish to provide it, move on.

Prime lenders offer lower rates with lower fees but have strict credit guidelines. You cannot have any late payments on any mortgage or loan within the last 24 months. You can have a front-end debt ratio of 36 percent, which is the mortgage payment alone, even up to 50 percent or greater for back-end debt, which includes the mortgage and all other liabilities, with excellent credit over 720, for PITI plus monthly expenses. If you do have a few late payments, you may still get a prime lender to give you a loan but your rate will usually be higher. If you have a large equity base in the home you are buying or a large amount of cash assets, you can usually offset a penalty, so check into this. If you have an overall favorable credit history, you should be placed in a prime loan. If the rate or requirements sound too stringent, ask what kind of loan they are placing you in. You will absolutely know the difference.

Subprime lending has become more popular. Approval is far easier, and even if you have had a bankruptcy or foreclosure in the last few months, you can often get a mortgage. You can avoid PMI insurance with a subprime mortgage because prime lenders require a loan to value ratio of 80 percent or less, meaning you must have 20 percent equity in the home. In some ways, subprime loans are made without any regard for the borrower's ability to repay the loan. They often have heavy prepayment penalties, credit insurance, and carry higher rates. Understandably, there are many excellent credit risk borrowers that go into subprime loans, as a result of a medical condition, divorce, or extended job loss that causes a credit score to drop significantly. If this is your specific case, take this type of loan on a one- to three-year basis if it immediately helps solve another issue, while helping you re-establish yourself. Remember that the mortgage is merely a tool. Tools need to be changed out and maintained on a regular basis.

Financing a Foreclosure with Less-Than-Stellar Credit

If you have less-than-stellar credit, you're going to pay for it through higher interest rates, sometimes a higher down payment, and perhaps up-front fees. Look for subprime lending, as noted above. However, less-than stellar credit does not mean that you cannot get a loan and it does not mean you cannot buy a foreclosure. Remember that another important area to securing a loan is your debt-to-income ratio, and the loan-to-value ratio on the home. Credit score is a tremendous indicator, though not all-inclusive. If you can validate your income and/or assets, there should be a lesser impact on the pricing that you'll be looking at. Another important factor will depend on whether you have, or will utilize, a down payment. Contrary to popular belief, you may finance a foreclosure with no money down, if your credit, income, and assets support your ability to do so. You may, however, not like the payment.

A recent client in Bill's portfolio had a 520 credit score (huge risk) due to large amounts of consumer debt (even worse), but was still able to get decent pricing on a subprime loan for two years—enought time to get their credit re-established.

Based on the above-mentioned items, the lender will care about your debt ratio. This is an important indicator of your ability to repay the mortgage. This is calculated by taking the monthly debts (housing expenses for your new loan plus other monthly expenses) and dividing it by the total monthly income. If your obligations monthly are $2,000 for the new fore-closure home you are trying to buy and $1,000 for your car and other obligations, you owe $3,000 per month. If you earn $6,000 per month, your debt ratio is $3,000 divided by $6,000, or 50 percent. The lower the debt ratio the better your mortgage rate will be. In some instances, you will not be able to borrow with a high debt ratio. This may be an instance where credit history may be as important as your credit score. In order to allow a higher debt-to-income ratio, the lender must feel that there are enough supporting "compensating factors" to ensure you can make the payment, and will not default during the first few months.

Your interest rate, as already mentioned, also depends on your credit score. It depends on the loan-to-value of the home (the value versus how much you want the bank to lend you), and your general credit (bankruptcies, loan history, and other public records). Bear in mind that if you want to buy the property with no money down, to the lender this is the riskiest loan they can possibly write. Presuming that you cannot verify income, assets, employment, and any other items, you will not receive the most favorable of terms, particularly those that are often promoted online. For this reason, we highly recommend (throughout the book) that you go in prepared with some kind of down payment. You can always take a second mortgage or equity line out against the home after you've closed escrow, made some improvements, and received a higher appraised value. It just becomes an additional source of investment money when you've done a few of these purchases, and have access to your own money.

Paper Rating

Your loan will be given a "paper rating." This is essentially a grade, and the grade will determine your interest rate. If all four of the factors noted above are outstanding, you will have an A paper. If just one element isn't great, you may be downgraded to an A- (or what is now called Alternative A paper), a B, a C or even a D paper. A D paper is the worst type and is usually based entirely on equity and not on your credit.

Any lender who gives money to a B, C, or D loan is taking more risk because there is a greater chance you will not pay back your loan. The lender is compensated for that risk by charging you more interest. A- papers may, for instance, pay 1 percent to 1.75 percent higher than A papers. B may pay .25 to .75 percent higher than A-, C .75 to 1.5 percent more than Bs, and Ds 1 to 1.75 percent higher than Cs. This varies *greatly* from lender to lender; however, it is a good general rule to follow (Mortgage-X). In summary, if you are looking at a 30-year fixed rate at a fair market rate of 6.00 percent based on an A paper rating, it would not be unusual to see a 12.00 interest rate or higher based on a D paper rating. This can become a painful difference in the monthly payment. You need to understand these scoring systems, as it will greatly affect your ability to purchase several foreclosure properties. Once you purchase a property, realizing the cost savings and instant equity, you will want to purchase more.

We researched what most organizations use, and found Mortgage-X issues a credit rating guide, available on the internet at http://mortgage-x.com/library/credit_grade.htm. In it is the table below, which shows how

Credit Grade Guide

Grade	Credit Score	Debt Ratio	Max LTV	Delinquencies w/in last 12 months	Credit Mortgage	Installment	Revolving	Bankruptcy/Foreclosure
A+ to A	670+	36-38	95-100	30 days	0	0-1	1-2	Good/excellent credit during last 2-5 years. No mortgage lates within 24 months. No bankruptcy within the last 2-10 years.
				60 days	0	0	0-1	
A-	650	45	95	30 days	0-1	1-2	2-3	No 60-day mortgage lates. Minimum 24-48 months since bankruptcy discharge.
				60 days	0	0-1	0-2	
B+ to B-	620	50	75-85	30 days	1-2	2-4	3-5	24-48 months since bankruptcy discharge. Re-established credit.
				60 days	0-1	1-2	1-2	
C+ to C-	580	55	75	30 days	3-4	4-6	5-7	12-24 months since bankruptcy discharge.
				60 days	0-2	2-4	3-5	
D+ to D-	550	60	65-70	60 days	1-3	5-7	6-8	Bankruptcy discharged within last 12 months.
				Poor payment record with limited 90-day, isolated 120-day lates.				
E	520-	65	50-65	Poor payment record with a pattern of 30, 60, and 90+ lates				Possible current bankruptcy or foreclosure. Stable current employment.

defaults and credit impacts your score and your rate. Please note that this is just a general guideline.

When you first approach a bank for pre-qualification, be sure to ask where you fit into the categories. Use the table to give you an idea; this will help you negotiate with banks.

Credit and Home Value

Here's a snapshot of how credit is tied to the appraised value of the home. While the loan-to-value ratio on foreclosures is generally very good, as you typically purchase them below the market or appraised value, you should be aware that the general rule of thumb is to lend on the lower of the purchase price, or the appraised value. This means that while the property is worth a lot more than you are paying for it, the difference is built-in equity, but will not change the manner of financing.

For example, a client recently purchased a bank-owned property in California for $560,000. The transaction was financed as a no-money-down deal, with a first mortgage of 80 percent of the value of the home and a corresponding 20 percent second mortgage. The property appraised at $625,000 so this client has $65,000 worth of equity. He's making significant improvements to the property, and will have the ability to refinance the property six months after purchasing it with a much better loan to value, as the home is located in an area with much higher priced homes.

Finding the Right Lender for your Foreclosure

There are two ways to get a loan if credit is a concern. The first is called Direct to Lender, or "DTL," which basically means you are going directly to the bank and not through a mortgage broker. There are lots of banks that deal with C- and D-rated paper; there are even some banks that work with E paper; you will pay a heavy interest penalty, but it is doable. If you find out you are a C- or D-rated loan, do an internet search for "D-rated mortgage" and find lenders that specialize in this type of paper.

Historically, direct lenders are the best way to go. But as the frenzy of the market is over, the same direct lenders that offered the best deals are tightening their rates and margins and starting to charge higher rates than mortgage banks or mortgage brokers. This should not occur in a well-balanced marketplace, but the contraction in the marketplace is causing even major companies such as WaMu, Bank of America, Chase, and Countrywide to tighten their lending belts, partly in hopes of keeping Wall Street happy with their financial performance

If you feel absolutely stuck, or just have very complicated finances, consider a mortgage broker. Mortgage brokers are given a different price than is given to a consumer, known as a wholesale price. The mortgage broker has lots of loan options because they deal with many lenders. Sometimes if you have tricky credit or really need to have access to lots of banks, this is a viable option. You can find a mortgage broker that deals with less-than-stellar credit and still have your foreclosure financed.

We recommend staying away from mortgage brokers, as while a few—very few—are helpful, most are just charging you interest and points that you do not need to pay. This is how they make their money. Go DTL if at all possible. You can research the types of loan programs available to you and eliminate the need to work with a mortgage broker that puts their needs above yours.

I'm not a fan of mortgage brokers. While some are honest, they all make money by adding costs to the consumer! Some practices border on unethical and some are even illegal. Often, they prey on those who do not understand the mortgage process or have really bad credit. These same individuals can go directly to the lender themselves and not pay yield spread, extra points, or any other markup the broker charges to make money. Mortgage brokers say that they help the person by walking them through the loan—so will a lender! I personally see no value add in mortgage brokering and don't think it's a business with longevity. In some cases mortgage brokers add to the time it takes to get things done, ultimately cost the consumer more, and pay low-wage people to help them with clients that don't understand the concepts of finance, debt consolidation, tax benefits, etc. I recommend to everyone that they go directly to lenders unless they have a friend in the mortgage brokering business they are sure won't charge them more.

—Dani

Take the opportunity to research your initial choices online. When you do, include all of the correct criteria such as credit score, income, and any other items that will need to be verified, or you'll be comparing apples to oranges. When you feel comfortable with what payments will look like, based on the price of the foreclosure asset, you can speak with your choice of lenders, knowing that you are well informed. At this point, as an educated consumer, you will not fall prey to the lenders who have become accustomed to charging excessive fees—typically, the mortgage brokers or bankers.

Author's Notes

I also believe that many mortgage bankers and brokers are nothing more than used car salesman, trying to see how much pain they can inflict upon you (in the form of excessive fees) as when you are haggling to purchase a vehicle. For too long, the mortgage industry relied on the frenzied marketplace; now that the market has normalized, competition and experience once again takes over. During this "downturn," my business has almost tripled by providing customized solutions, which often include a recommendation to not refinance or even purchase a property that may not make financial sense. I am enjoying the ability to provide the direct-to-lender formula of lower costs and lower rates to the mortgage banker and broker community; I can say others are taking note. I'm dealing with lenders and brokers who are genuinely upset that I have exposed their deceptive practices of charging excessive fees to any individual who does not know any better.

—Bill

Before continuing, we want to point out a tool that we use often. It is First Franklin's Glossary, which provides a definition of lots of the most common mortgage terms that you and your lender will work with. The more educated you are on the process, the better you will be able to speak their language and secure a good deal. You can find this online at www.ff.com/public/glossary.jsp. Additionally, we have included a list of common terms at the end of the book, provided by the LandAmerica Financial Group, some or all of which may be duplicated. If you are confused by the bank you're using or feel tempted to use a broker who will "ease you through the process," spend half an hour on this site, at the very least taking the time to read through some of these terms. You'll feel more informed and better capable of handling the transaction. For purposes of confidentiality, the policies discussed will not be attached to any specific organization, though you should know they are commonplace. Read on for more.

The Future of Mortgage Banking

Every industry has seen its trends and the internet has forever changed the way every business handles its share of the market. In the great housing boom of the late 90s and early 2000s, lenders came up with all types of unique, innovative loan programs to help fund loans for homes that were appreciating, and thereby securing the bank's money. So what does the future of mortgage banking hold? We foresee added loan programs (think 50-year mortgage), changing markets, and perhaps even fewer players in the marketplace due to increased competition, especially from big banks with the money to invest in technology.

At press time, two major institutions, Bank of America and Countrywide, are discussing an initial strategic alliance, culminating in a potential merger with the latter company. With bank consolidations, as well as the volumes of information provided on the internet, smaller banks and mortgage brokers may be less likely to loan money in the future. This is an overall positive occurrence as attrition will drive the poorer performers, whether individuals or organizations, out of the business.

The bigger institutions with outsourced processes and online applications will take hold. For example, many big banks outsource their appraisal processes, send loan processing or underwriting overseas, and do most of their paperwork—including closings—entirely electronically. In our opinion, e-mortgages and e-signing—the entire process being done on the internet—will be commonplace in the next decade. Due to the complexity of real estate transactions, real estate in general has been one of the slowest service sectors to go fully automated, but it is only a matter of time. Moving forward, banks are going to have to spend an enormous amount of money protecting the privacy and security of individual data through high-level encryption. It is our prediction that small banks and small mortgage brokers will not be able to compete in this type of marketplace. Automated valuation is going to continue to be a key in cutting lender costs and increasing the accuracy of risk assessment, and even satellites (think Google Earth) are playing a role—for instance, using them to verify a house is really on the parcel the paperwork says it is.

(Yes, Bill has seen an escrow and title companies provide information for the wrong parcel number to be financed!)

The big push will be to increase margins for the lender, and decrease costs for the consumer. This is the "natural way" when information becomes transparent, which the internet has no doubt enabled. We're also going to see a big push for searching online and the ability to integrate; to integrate your banking information into one platform, to ensure timely payments, to set up automatic reminders and many other tools.

> **Author's Notes**
>
> Bank of America is already allowing its online banking customers to set all sorts of electronic alerts, from bills being due to direct deposits hitting their accounts. This will be expanded upon greatly in the coming years; expect to see more new products come to market in the next 18 months.

Software companies will continue to web-enable existing technology and create new web-based platforms that can integrate multiple aspects of the lending process. What does this mean for you the consumer? Easier, faster, simplified, lower-cost transactions.

As we see growth in the market slow, we'll also see margins shrink and competition increase online. This means that lenders are going to have to become more efficient, which all but guarantees a push to technology. While we are on the cusp of achieving this now, some major banks have recently made a push to increase their margins by allowing their loan originators to charge an "overage" of up to one point, which is split with the bank. This overage typically raises the interest rate by approximately one half of one point, which of course in turn benefits the lending institution that wants and needs to make more money, as long as the public face of the institution stays within fair-lending regulations. Know what you're dealing with, and you'll feel like you're an employee of the lender that will be assured the best deal possible.

Media Hype?

No doubt you've heard rumblings lately in the media about falling home prices, the "housing bubble," and even appalling comparisons to the dot-com stock bubble. The facts couldn't be further from the truth. We firmly believe that real estate is different than stocks. You can see, touch, and feel this asset. Handled properly, your ownership of one or many foreclosure properties will provide a benefit to those individuals and families who are not fortunate enough to purchase a property of their own just yet. While stocks provide their own income stream, stocks do not provide an area for families to grow together, shelter for family, or a place to call home. While several factors, including unemployment rates, interest rates, supply, demand, and inflation all affect the housing market, the market has historically (over a relatively moderate period of time) never gone down.

It is our opinion that the media enjoys reporting bad news because it boosts ratings, but it is not necessarily accurate. One of Bill's favorite real estate economists, Gary Watts, makes satirical references to all of the major media events in the last few years that include, but are not limited to, Y2K, SARS, killer bees, and bird flu, to name a few, that always appear much larger than they really are. In fact, other than a few business shows, we find errors in reporting and statistical manipulation all the time. One of the authors of this book teaches doctoral statistics and can say without a doubt that much of the information you get as a consumer is distorted.

This should help you feel more comfortable with buying foreclosures. While neither of us can ever predict the market or pretend to know what is good for an individual consumer or investor, we do know we're both bullish on the market both short and long term, and we've done well investing in it—including throughout the recent "downward trend" market. If anything, this current market for the next few years should prove to be a great time to invest. Both of us are doing it, not just talking about it.

Beyond the Bubble

The housing "bubble" isn't the only thing we feel the media is hyping. The media often slams the negative amortization mortgages we talked about earlier as the "reason most people will go into foreclosure." Most?

Not quite. Sure, default rates will be higher, but banks have accounted for that risk. It will create bargains all around! Not to say that overly creative loans have not contributed to some degree, but the real issue lies in a borrower's ability (or inability) to understand what they can and cannot afford, combined with the fact that these mortgages add to the balance. A real estate agent was recently annoyed with Bill's honest conversation with a borrower and their ability to handle the payment. Ask yourself why an 80-year-old gentleman on a pension and Social Security income would purchase a home with no money down and limited assets. If he agreed to write that loan, he should just have a sign-up sheet for individuals willing to buy the property as a foreclosure. A week later, the same agent requests assistance on a similar transaction. After interviewing the borrower, they commented that they did not believe they could ever be faced with such a difficult situation of not being able to pay their mortgage; "Do you have anyone that can buy the property from us? We cannot continue this way." In their nine months of ownership, they added $13,500 to their balance, had $4,000 in reserves when they bought the property, with a 590 credit score at the time, yet were approved with no money down. Do you blame the program, or the unethical agent and lender that put them there?

Time to Buy

The market is certainly changing. As we see more foreclosures come to market, from the pre-foreclosure stage to the formal notice of default, ultimately resulting in an auction or even a bank-owned property, that inventory will be used up, being bought first since it will be priced cheaper (increased supply). This will result in a shift to a more conservative lending system and greater risk management with yet again another housing boom (increasing demand).

This is of course is only our prediction, based on our experience in the marketplace, understanding of the underlying factors causing the change, and the natural shift in the real estate cycle. Ideally, this is the time to buy foreclosures as the banks will do everything possible to avoid a meltdown similar to the "aerospace driven meltdown" in the late '80s and early '90s; it will only get better from an investment perspective (of course, not if you're the individual in foreclosure) throughout the coming couple of years as negative amortization and interest only loans begin to amortize.

Loss Mitigation

Banks are in the business of making money, not losing it. While it seems like a simple equation, where the banks do a really good job of assessing risk overall and charging for it appropriately (in their favor of course), the bank is going to take some hits and will incur some loss. Aside from fraudulent activity, and even under the most optimistic of scenarios, these defaults tend to occur within the first eighteen months of the loan. Their goal is to lessen the loss, or mitigate it, through their loss mitigation process and in some banks, loss mitigation departments.

How Banks are Minimizing Risk

To help minimize the potential risk and to offset the increase in foreclosures or bank-owned real estate that we'll see in the coming years, banks are creating new loss mitigation techniques. They are moving towards a more automated method of providing appraisals and they are requiring greater validation of the information being provided. They are creating stiffer interest penalties for no-doc loans, requiring higher down payment amounts based on lower incomes, and assets to support a greater reserve requirement equal to six to twelve month's worth of payments. Loss mitigation departments have already begun hiring "consultants" that are not part of the "collection" arm of these departments; their sole purpose is to see if they can facilitate a forbearance (deferment of payments), or any other arrangement that helps the consumer keep their home.

Incentives

Conversely, even more creative programs are being offered as an incentive for higher credit scores and significant assets. The larger institutional brokerages that have typically invested in mortgage-backed securities are now providing mortgage money, in a sense redefining the normal loss mitigation programs by the more popular lenders. Your goal is to understand the thinking and methodology so that you can work within their framework in purchasing properties at a significant discount.

Appraisals in the Loan Process

The appraisal market has been somewhat "sketchy." We use this term loosely, because it is meant solely to describe the inconsistency between appraisers, whether they have had a good or a bad day, who does the appraisal, what company they work for, and that company's practices. Appraisals have held up numerous loan deals on homes that were perfectly fine and should have been valuing higher. There have also been instances where over-appraising a home has led to foreclosure and increased bank risk. Appraisals also reflect previous sales—not future sales—and that is what is needed to properly appraise a property.

Interestingly, appraisers have commented to Bill that they would provide a higher value based on closed sales, but cannot as they see the market turning for the worse, though there is absolutely no data to support this view. This is an excellent example of an appraiser who fails to understand their fiduciary duty to the borrower as well to the bank. They were advised by the bank to err on the side of being conservative, so they felt they should lower the value *ahead* of the marketplace. As a result, many companies are moving towards an automated appraisal system. However, this too has numerous flaws. Namely, this approach looks at a cost per square foot, and nothing more, as it fails to address upgrades, custom work, and any level of quality improvements in the home being appraised. This system works great with significant down payments where a visual appraisal is not necessary. Individuals are often willing to pay more for a move-in ready home.

Some people believe that inaccurate appraisals and appraisers getting "high" off of an inflated market has hurt the banks and has created a situation leading to higher foreclosure rates. Appraisals, as we discuss in detail later, have a significant impact on both your ability to fund a new loan and your ability to sell a house once you own it. Some banks are relying on tighter appraisers and even in-house appraisers that work for the bank and will err on the side of conservative estimates to help them reduce their risk. At the same time, the contraction in the marketplace has caused some major lenders to completely outsource their appraisal processes to fee appraisers and outside contractors, so they can eliminate the cost associated with salaries and benefits. This is often bad for the homeowners as they're left with properties that have lower appraisals than they are actually worth, based on old data, and they must come up with the difference to meet loan-to-value requirements with cash they may not have. We are not convinced that more conservative appraising will fix the problem; perhaps greater consumer education about loan types will. By the same token, we believe that as you will purchase homes with a significant level of equity, the appraisal will not be as important as you may believe, but as indicated, the loan program will be of huge importance.

Freddie Mac has recently introduced "rescue products" to protect the economic impact that foreclosures may have across the U.S. These programs are designed to assist families throughout all states. Fannie Mae, on the other hand, has tightened its lending standards moving forward.

Finding the facts

Borrower-Hired Appraisers

Lots of people ask us if they can use their own appraisers. Banks tend to have a list of appraisers that they have approved; if your appraiser isn't on it, the answer will be a flat "No!" However if the appraiser is on it, you might want to pay for your own appraisal (if you know the appraiser), and then give the appraisal to the bank. Find out first if the bank will accept it before you go to the expense. Usually from there, they simply have their own group review it to make sure it looks accurate. Often, you can get a more accurate appraisal this way. Since banks are erring on the side of conservatism (to an extreme in some cases), this may be your best opportunity for an accurate appraisal that both you and the bank can live with.

As with any professional, appraisers are both licensed and certified. They are commonly monitored by the state, and dread the possibility of being reported for poor judgment, or even worse, fraud. Bill had an appraisal on a personal property come in significantly below the purchase price. Knowing that he was protected contractually with dual contingencies, it seemed like the only option the builder had was to drop the price accordingly. The builder chose a more difficult path by challenging the initial appraisal, ordering one of their own. Not surprisingly, the second appraisal, which was ordered by the builder at their own discretion, came in right at the purchase price. Having noted several inconsistencies, the builder's appraisal was called into question, along with letting the builder know he would hold him complicit to commit fraud if he used that specific appraisal. The second appraisal ordered by the builder at his guidance came in lower than the second, but higher than the independent appraisal ordered. It is important to read through the data, if for no other reason than to become informed as to the process by which the properties are appraised. Had he not been in the business, he would have merely been told the purchase price came in as expected, and the builder would never have said a thing. This transaction has now entered into legal mediation per the terms of the contract because an acceptable solution could not be found. Remember that the appraisal is designed to

> **Author's Notes**
>
> We recommend that you be cautious of appraisers that are friends with small bankers. When one of the authors was buying a home in a particular city, the author got a great appraisal and was able to proceed with the loan, a rather expensive loan in fact. The author needed this particular loan closed quickly due to time constraints and was willing to pay the higher price of this bank. Three months later, when the author went to refinance the home, the same appraiser came back with an appraisal a full $50,000 lower than the first time! There was no way the home dropped in price that fast, so it quickly became apparent that the appraiser was probably a less-than-honest one. The new bank had to use this new appraisal and the author's rates shot up. The lesson here? Find someone you trust, someone that is fair, and someone that is accurate. Just like the bank does not want to take uncalculated risks, you shouldn't want to either. Do not find appraisers that over-inflate because it will hurt you in the long run. Keeping everything precise and accurate is always best.

protect your investment in the property, as well as the bank's interest in case of future default or foreclosure. More often than not, the appraised value on a bank-owned property or foreclosure will be higher than what you are paying for it. However, do not be amazed that the appraisal reflects the price you are paying for the property, and not the built-in equity. This is a common tactic used by appraisers so they are not accused of over- or undervaluing properties.

Why Banks Do Not Want to Own Property

As with any business, banks need to make a profit; they need to show shareholder value and offer a return on investment. Banks make money by lending money at a higher interest rate than they pay out. Banks can only do this if owners continue to make interest payments, and continue to give the bank money that it can then reinvest for a higher rate of return. This is why many banks are getting into riskier loans—they are able to charge more, reinvest that money (even if the owner only pays for a short while), and then loan it out at a higher rate. To do this, banks also need a good balance of solid loans that will pay consistently to give them a base of money and income that they can take at least part of and loan it out to higher-risk individuals that will pay a greater return.

Additionally, one must understand that the bank or lender issuing the mortgage is doing it typically for what is known as "servicing rights," which include the collection of payments, escrow account management, foreclosure proceedings, and other fees. The mortgage-backed security is sold to Fannie Mae, Freddie Mac, or private and institutional investors. A common approach would be to sell a pool of 30-year fixed-rate mortgages at 6.5 percent, sold at a discount of 6.25 percent to the investment community, resulting in the ability of the bank to keep the servicing rights.

If the bank ends up owning the property, they do not make money, as the interest for the owner continues to accumulate against the account, in addition to the cost of attorneys, legal proceedings, and all of the correspondent research of foreclosing on the property. Their goal is not to own property—and this is one reason you should contact your bank immediately if you are going to be late with your payment. Believe it or not, both the owner and the bank have the same goal—for you to continue making your monthly payments and paying them interest, so they can take that money (minus reserve requirements) and lend it out to others who will pay even more for it.

The Logic Behind Banks Not Wanting to Own Property

When the bank has to foreclose on a property, it costs them a lot of money. They must go through the foreclosure process (perhaps even through the courts, depending on the state), they must get their legal team involved, they have to pay for lots of phone calls and customer service time, not to mention the broker that eventually sells the home and even perhaps the auction. If interest rates have dropped, the bank is going to lose out on a person paying, say, 8 percent to someone who will buy the home at a new, perhaps lower rate. The property also may have been financed for more than it is now worth, since the home may have deteriorated or devalued. It is clearly better for the bank to continue earning interest than to own the home.

There are also regulations that govern the amount of bad debt a bank can carry on its books and the amount of money it must have in reserves. Owning property impacts each of these elements. As a result, lenders will often settle with you directly via a short sale, where they accept a lesser amount than what is owed, rather than going through the entire foreclosure process. The best situation you can be in if you want to short-sell the property directly with the bank is for the bank to hold a bigger note in the property than its most likely worth. Realize that purchasing a short sale typically requires employing a real estate agent experienced in handling short sale transactions. There is a completely different approach to handling these transactions, which generally take 45-60 days to close if all the parties cooperate in the paperwork that is requested and required to handle the short sale correctly.

A short sale has the ability to decrease the banks' liability because if the home goes to auction, they

The bank continues to accumulate interest, as an expense, according to the original terms of the loan when dealing with bank-owned property. It is important to know how long a property has been on a bank's balance sheet, as they will be more motivated to sell the homes that have been on record for longer periods of time.

Finding the facts

may lose even more. Having said this, the seller must have permission from the bank, who will scrutinize why they should allow the seller to settle for less than what is owed, which in turn benefits you as the buyer by providing a lower price point with built-in equity. Also, if there is a large second mortgage holder, they are at risk because they know the first mortgage holder is foreclosing. This is one of the primary reasons for the higher interest on second mortgages, as they must account for the added level of risk if the mortgages default, understanding they are in a subordinate, or secondary position. You may be able to short sell the second note holder, and they clearly know it. Again, as a buyer or investor, this greatly benefits you. Do not expect the bank to readily acknowledge this.

Offers on Short Sales

If you decide to make an offer to the bank on a short sale, please remember that the process of valuing the property is different and you want to be included in it. Here's how it works.

The Appraisal

The lender will get a Broker's Price Opinion, or BPO. A real estate agent that is hired by the lender evaluates the property and suggests a price.

You want the agent to come down as low as possible. You want the lender to let you know when the agent will be at the home and try to get him or her to come in with a low value. Show up there with a list of every repair and estimate for the property, even if you have to get a contractor to bid a job or repair. Come with a list of comparable sales (the lower ones). Sometimes the agents will ask why you are there; just tell them that you are the buyer and you need to know what the price will be. It does not hurt to tell the agent the price you need to buy the home for, and then call a day or two later to see if you "got the price you needed." Since you have no control over this process or the person, you want them to come in low and you will try to encourage them, but it is really up to them. If you are selling the house, do not forget to take your "for sale" sign in! If someone is still living there, ask him or her to leave when the agent comes out. You want the house to look as low in value as possible, so unlike with traditional sales, it's okay if the house is a mess and looking less than livable.

Finding the facts

Short sales are worthy investments, but require a high level of patience, as they often involve 45 days to 3 months to close, in the absence of advance preparation on the part of the buyer or investor.

Owner-Occupied vs. Investor

If you are a buyer who intends to occupy the home, even if you decided to purchase a short sale, you need a contract with the seller, so still go through those steps. But do understand why the bank does not want to hold the property—which is good for you, the home bargain hunter. Be aware that different rules apply to short sales if you are an investor. An experienced real estate broker or agent can guide you. Typically, there are very few agents that can handle these transactions without really worsening the situation. Bill has dealt with some transactions that had to be completely rewritten and repackaged for the "short-sale" lender to approve. In several states, an agent cannot be involved in the short-sale process to an investor, except as a referring agent to the bank. You must be very patient in these transactions, which will pay off if you provide a solution to the bank by purchasing a short-sale property.

The Final Details on Short Sales

Before you call the bank, be sure that you get permission in writing from the owner, using an Authorization to Release and Convey Information form, as the bank will not speak to you under any circumstance without this clearance from the seller. There really is no way around this. The Loss Mitigation Department will handle this transaction from beginning to end. Be firm and thorough, but be nice. It is very easy to move your file to the bottom of the stack if you attempt to play hardball with this department.

Remember that as the bank attempts to get the defaulted property off of its books, it will go through the process of notice of default, the notice of trustee sale, or the real estate owned phase. Be sure you know which stage the property is in at all times. The bank's desire to dump the property will be largely dependent on this.

Bank's Liquidation—Your Gain!

We have mentioned the process that banks go through to get rid of the risk that banks have by holding onto property and the potential negative effects it has on their books. You already know that banks go through a process to liquidate inventory that they must carry to pay off liens. Their liquidation is, of course, your gain! If you choose to endeavor in pre-foreclosures or full-blown REOs, you will, more often than not, make money in doing so. The equity savings is built in, as the banks know it is necessary to provide a discount to move the property. Unlike the frenzied days in 2003 and 2004, where homes were resold with multiple counteroffers and the default ratio was close to non-existent, most foreclosure properties have a fair amount of equity built in. Did you know though that banks actually have departments throughout their organizations designed to mitigate this potential risk in the first place? Understanding them is one element to knowing how to get a good deal.

Bank Departments and Duties

We have mentioned briefly Loss Mitigation Departments. There are lots of departments within the banks and lenders that handle various aspects of the process of foreclosure and pre-foreclosure. If you originate a loan through Bank of America, WaMu, Countrywide or World Savings, they will typically retain the servicing rights because of their client base and mix of business. With other lenders, such as Chase, Citibank, GMAC, Wells Fargo, and several mortgage brokers, you have a greater chance that your loan will be resold, often times to each other. Many of these organizations will handle the transaction internally up to the default process, where they will outsource the remainder of the collection process, including the formal foreclosure to an outside organization. Follow the trail, so you do not waste time trying to hunt a property down through the wrong channels.

We're going to explain now what each of the departments at the banks do, and whom you need to speak with and when.

Underwriters

Many of us know the word "underwriter" because we often perceive them as the ones holding up our loans. Often, they are! It is their job to make sure that everything is in order before letting a loan fund or, in some cases, even allowing docs to be issued on the loan. Every bank has mortgage underwriting guidelines for each type of loan. The underwriter has ultimate responsibility for verifying all of them, if the processor does not have the signing authority to clear the specific condition that has been requested of the borrower. Underwriters often verify information, request documentation, and "clear a file" to close, and sometimes in extreme circumstances will prevent a deal from closing. It is the underwriter's responsibility to help the bank mitigate risk by looking at any-

Finding the facts

Underwriters are the front-line defense for banks in preventing future defaults. While their position is to help in structuring a loan successfully, their position has quickly morphed into looking for reasons NOT to approve a loan if it represents a risk to the lender.

thing "fishy" in the deal (for example, if you have five "second homes"), they may verify income, they may ask for tax statements and other documents.

Depending on the company and its leadership and approach to lending, the underwriter is supposed to find a way to approve the deal; regrettably, the underwriters have supreme authority that more often than not is specifically looking for reasons not to write the deal. They truly possess the magic pen, and the attitude to go along with it.

At this point, experience is critical. The real estate and lending industry is closely knit among the high producing performers. Their reputation is on the line, so most will do everything to challenge an underwriter, assuming that you can convince the person originating the loan. While not defending underwriters, they clearly do receive deals from inexperienced originators, lenders, and brokers that lack any resemblance of a complete loan package, so they become a little jaded. These individuals receive a base salary, and a significant bonus for approving loans. They also are immediately investigated if they write too many deals that default during an initial phase of the loan. Let's just say that they are trained to sniff out the faults in the loan, regardless of how minor those faults may be. As well-prepared buyers and investors, do everything in your power to prepare so your file will never end up in front of an underwriter for lack of preparation and information.

> *Author's Note*
>
> Underwriters may serve a purpose, but they can be a serious pain. Dani has had more loans held up by underwriters that cannot think their way out of a wet paper bag than just about anyone else (other than mortgage brokers). Some are good and do their job well, but others just add headaches to the process. If you have a loan that is atypical (perhaps you get income from passive sources or you are a contractor), expect delays. The underwriters can really put processes on hold and cause a lot of grief! Make sure your lender has a good rapport with the underwriter as this may help make things go more smoothly.

Loss Mitigation Departments

Loss Mitigation Departments do precisely what their name implies; their job is to reduce the chances of loss for the bank. It is nearly impossible to short sell a home without involving this department. Short selling, again, is getting the bank to sell a home to you for less than what is owed—in some cases, far less. Loss Mitigation is a "working out" department, the department that handles foreclosures, short sales, loan modifications, and reinstatements. You may have to ask for any of these departments for the general operator to know what you're looking for, so be specific when you phone. Remember you'll need to fax an "authorization to release information" form to them, so get their name, direct number, and fax number.

Once you've sent the document, you can begin discussing your deal with them. We recommend that you personalize your discussion by referring to the homeowner by name as often as possible; do not come across looking like a greedy investor! Be sure to follow up with the rep you speak to, and be friendly. Also find out who makes the decisions in these situations and how long it takes. The loss mitigation rep at some companies has the ability to help push through deals. Note that loss mitigation is usually different from the collections department, which is often where you'll be routed (perhaps many times) in an attempt to collect debt—even though you do not owe it. Be persistent and explain what you're looking for and who you want to talk to.

Bank Asset Manager

A bank asset manager is typically the final signature required in the short sale and/or foreclosure process. Rarely will you ever reach this individual, as they are highly insulated from the public. Part of this lack of visibility is that there are few asset managers within certain organizations. While reasonable at times, they often times look at the transaction from the standpoint of the insurance company that typically provides the mortgage insurance against the home. If this individual does not like the deal, it will not happen. Depending on the institution, most of the banks cover their mortgages with lender-paid mortgage insurance that protects them against default. For example, a mortgage with a 100 percent loan-to-value may have 35 percent mortgage insurance coverage, meaning that the risk has been spread to an outside insurance company; at 90 percent loan-to-value it will have 25 percent mortgage insurance coverage; at 85 percent loan-to-value, the bank will have 12 percent coverage. While the asset manager does not negotiate these percentages, they ensure the ability to stay within the guideline, so most of the risk is spread to an outside insurance company in the case of default. Generally, a break even point for a mortgage is around 70 percent, meaning that the bank will typically not sell below this range; this should give you an idea how low you will be able to go, but do not expect this amount to be volunteered to you, especially if you are new at the foreclosure investment game.

> Asset managers in banks may be the least understood position, but they have an important role in managing the bank's risk.
>
> *Finding the facts*

This will be a back and forth process, until you know all of the players involved in the process. Do not get visibly frustrated throughout the transaction; your patience will be rewarded. If you are a control freak, this will not be the most ideal way to invest, though the rewards are great when dealing with the asset manager's staff. These are great friends to have; they know EVERYTHING related to their bank's foreclosure assets. Recently, a difficult agent was working with a major lender, and commented how over the last two months they had so much difficulty putting a deal together as the lender was so difficult. Ironically, Bill called the same company and was able to negotiate a new deal within ten days. This individual lacked experience and the asset manager was not satisfied with what was being provided. Too bad for that buyer! You can see clearly here why, after finding a foreclosure to buy, you're choosy in who you deal with.

There are also dedicated Asset Management companies that handle the inspections, appraisals, and any other foreclosure-related items for regional lenders, credit unions, and any other entity that is not large enough, or wants to handle their own foreclosure deals. They serve like a complete servicing and collection division for a collection of lenders.

Arbitration Managers

The Independent Arbitration Managers for smaller banks and lenders are individuals with a background in banking, real estate, and the finance industries that serve as contract workers with a high level of expertise. As the market continues to turn, some of these individuals may be placed on retainer with smaller regional banks and credit unions, as these specific organizations do not have enough consistent foreclosure activity to support having an individual on staff. Their goal is to protect the assets of the bank, while still keeping an objective viewpoint, as these individuals are not fully committed to the lending institution.

Appraisers

Last but certainly not least, it may seem odd to put appraisers in the Bank Departments and Duties section, but these days it isn't. Many banks have outsourced appraising and have appraisal review departments (or leave it to the underwriters), but some banks still have their own team of employees handling appraisals. Appraisers essentially determine the value of the home you are buying and as we noted in the above section, some lenders are counting on appraisers to help reduce the chance that they will lose money in a deal or that a home in foreclosure will not be worth what the appraiser estimated. We cannot begin to underscore the value of an appraisal, as this individual's failure to value the property accurately can result in delayed closings, and in certain circumstances, prevent the deal from closing at all.

For purposes of refinancing, appraisers will tend to the err on the side of a conservative value, so as to assure the bank they will not allow borrowers to lend more than a certain percentage of the home. For purposes of purchasing a property, whether an investment, foreclosure, or short sale, the appraisal is even more critical if only to help determine the equity position in the property, so you can ensure you are making a good purchase. If the property were to appraise below the purchase price, you would presumably receive the lower price, subject to any contractual obligations or contingencies that speak to the contrary. Since lending of properties is subject to the lower of purchase price or appraised value, a contract that does not address an appraisal contingency would mean you would need to have your down payment plus the deficiency between the purchase price and appraised value in order to close on the transaction.

You should be acutely aware that an appraisal is subjective and takes into account comparable values in the neighborhood along with a high level of research to help support the sales value of the home. In addition—and unfairly—it takes into account the appraiser's opinion. While this can be maddening, we've seen appraisals vary by 20 to 30 percent from appraiser to appraiser, or more! The entire appraisal process is flawed, as it is based on what someone else's home sold for X months ago, not what someone will buy for in 30 days from now. But until something new and better forecasts values, we're stuck with this poor model. Dani prefers Zillow's Zestimates as they take into account many factors, including upgrades.

In today's market, it is not unusual for properties of all types to appraise below the purchase price. If you spend a few hundred dollars for the appraisal and realize this occurs, simply walk away from the transaction, presuming the seller will not adjust their sales price. If the property appraises over value, you will know that the investment is well worth it. Again, our approach is to look at your acquisition of foreclosure properties as any other well-planned investments that makes sense and appreciates further over time. While you will have the opportunity to flip some properties, most of the time you will have opportunities for acquiring numerous rental properties that will create significant wealth in a two- to five-year time span, sometimes less, sometimes more.

FINDING
FORECLOSURES

THERE ARE LOTS OF WAYS TO FIND FORECLOSURES; SOME ARE COMPLEX and some very simple. In this chapter, we'll discuss most of the options that you have. Later in this book, in the chapter about partnerships, we'll go into detail about one organization making serious headway in their ability to bring foreclosures to the average consumer market. First, however, we'll outline some of the things that borrowers do to try to avoid foreclosure. Understanding this from the homeowner's perspective will help you understand what you're up against.

Avoiding Foreclosure

Homeowners have options to avoid foreclosures, and since banks do not want to own property or go through the hassles of selling it (often for less than the lien on the home), homeowners can take steps to avoid being foreclosed upon. These steps include:

- *Not* ignoring the collection letters from the bank
- Writing the bank's Loss Mitigation department (and being prepared to provide financial information)

- Staying in the home (homeowners may not qualify for assistance if they move out)
- Contacting a HUD-approved housing counseling agency.

Lenders will do all sorts of things to keep homes from being foreclosed upon, including:

- Issuing a special forbearance (a lender-approved repayment plan and even temporary suspension of payments)
- Mortgage modification (a refinance of the debt or an extension of the terms to lower the monthly payment)
- A partial claim (one-time payment from the FHA-insurance fund to bring your mortgage current that results in a promissory note issued as a lien against the property, interest free due when the home is sold or paid off)
- A pre-foreclosure sale (to avoid foreclosure by selling the property for less than the amount needed to pay off the loan)
- A deed-in-lieu of foreclosure (voluntarily giving back your property to the lender so as not to cause as much damage to your credit rating).

Owners may also choose to file for bankruptcy, though the home-owner may be stuck with bad credit for seven (or more) years and should seek the advice of an attorney before making such a radical decision. If you are at risk of a notice of default or foreclosure, you need to immediately take steps to consolidate where possible, refinance if necessary, or sell your home to avoid full foreclosure status where you will be left with nothing but a paid lien. As difficult as it may seem, lenders have a huge incentive to ensure that a borrower retains their home. This will be discussed in greater detail as we move forward; there are lots of resources out there to help you

Finding the facts

Mortgage fraud is on the rise. While it may be a cause of some foreclosures, it can also occur with investors who see the investment opportunity in a down market. Be cautious of how you invest if it means you have to cut corners. You will lose in the long run.

avoid foreclosure and you should seek them immediately if you begin to fall behind or even suspect that you will fall behind in the coming months. As an investor, you should be prepared to jump on these opportunities as they present themselves; the deal either works or it does not.

Keep Your Home: Everyone Wins

As we've learned, it is in the best interest of the bank and the homeowner to stay in the house, and all parties should do everything possible to maintain this relationship. And there are a lot of ways that banks help homeowners keep their homes. When an individual signs to buy a home, they are agreeing to make payments, to pay the bank back faithfully, and to give up their property should they be unable to keep that promise. This financial commitment is such that banks and lending institutions are taking a more aggressive approach in communicating with the borrower in making arrangements, as well as intervening as early as possible. Computer models exist that, similar to credit scores, can predict the possibility of a property owner falling behind in payments before the default actually occurs.

When a homeowner fails to make a payment, they are held responsible for giving up the collateral used to secure their loan—which usually means their home and even possibly their bank accounts. Recently, one of my borrowers was $180 past due on a home equity line of credit; even with an impeccable credit history, this caused their credit union to freeze their checking and savings accounts with aggregate balances over $10,000. The story sounded so farfetched that I called the collections department of the bank myself to verify the information. This should convince any homeowner that the lending institutions are serious about protecting their interest in the property.

It is imperative that a homeowner does everything possible to keep his or her home. Working with a good lender who understands the situation can be helpful, and sticking to a strict budget is absolutely necessary. Communicating with the lender is paramount to a successful outcome. It may appear embarrassing to make the phone call to one's lender or the respective servicing group to explain why one cannot make a payment, but the lender WANTS you to call. However, should arrangements not be made, or should the homeowner not qualify for arrangements by the bank, foreclosure proceedings may begin.

Avoid Scams: Keeping Yourself Out of Trouble

If you are the homeowner facing foreclosure, beware of numerous scams that will hurt you and could even land you in jail. If you are trying to acquire foreclosure property, you must do so legally—so read this section carefully so you know what you *cannot* do.

If you're the person interested in buying a foreclosure property, you *cannot* "equity skim." This is a scam in which the buyer approaches the homeowner offering to get them out of trouble by promising to pay off their mortgage or give the homeowner money when the home is sold. This approach has several variations, some of which include the real estate agent and finance people who agree to help the owner of the property. The buyer may suggest that the homeowner move out quickly and deed the property to the him or her, then the "buyer" collects rent and does not make any mortgage payments. This is called first payment default. Ultimately, the lender forecloses, the owner loses all of their equity and credit standing, and the FBI eventually investigates what occurred, as well as whether any laws were broken. If you are wondering why the FBI gets involved, remember that banks and most lending institutions are either federally regulated, and/or sell their mortgage-backed securities to federal agencies such as Fannie Mae and Freddie Mac.

As a homeowner, never sign over your deed unless it is part of your loan obligation. As a buyer, do not use this method to find foreclosures! It is not worth your time or investment attempting to circumvent the system by cheating others out of their homes and equity. You will have more than enough opportunities to maximize your investment by tapping into this new income stream.

As a homeowner, avoid phony counseling agencies. Some groups may refer to themselves as counseling agencies that handle various aspects of your situation for a fee, often doing things you can easily do yourself for free. Such things may be payment negotiations, a pre-foreclosure sale, or negotiating with the lender for time without payments. A recent client was contacted by a legitimate-sounding organization but, after following up, realized that the organization's own web site confirmed the need for a significant equity position. More often than not, this position of equity does not exist, as the current owner had used the home as a piggy bank, causing the cash-flow issues that resulted in the foreclosure action by the bank. Always call a HUD-approved housing counseling agency before you pay anyone or sign anything. The time the homeowner will spend on hold with HUD or researching on the internet will save them thousands of dollars and eliminate more unnecessary grief than one can ever imagine.

As a buyer, suggest that homeowners use HUD-approved housing counseling agencies as well. Just as Consumer Credit Counseling exists to help people with consumer and credit card debt, the Center for Responsible Lending can serve as a wonderful resource to guide someone in need of assistance. Additionally, several cities that offer Down Payment Assistance also offer recommendations on legitimate counseling agencies. As an investor, depending on the state that you live in, you could be violating certain laws by taking advantage of a homeowner who is seeking counseling or assistance to keep from losing their homes. By all means, stay on the right side of the law.

As a buyer, also be sure you never ask the homeowner to sign anything that they do not understand. Get all promises in writing, and beware of any contract of sale of loan assumption (an assumption that indicates the homeowner isn't released from the mortgage debt). Additionally, one should be aware that an assumption of mortgage will continue to report to the credit reporting agencies. It is risky and not typically recommended. If you intend to work directly with the seller, encourage the homeowner to obtain legal counsel. Not taking proper precautions and handling a home purchase that is about to go into foreclosure can get you into a difficult situation (HUD.gov). We want you to look at this as a smart and worthy investment, not a get-rich-quick scheme. Do your homework—you will have a higher propensity of creating and/or increasing your wealth if you are diligent in your research and execution.

Title Companies

Title companies not only play a role in helping to research a foreclosure once you've decided to make an offer, but they actually have information that will help you in the process of finding foreclosures. Often, title companies have the most accurate information because they pull it from public records, particularly county recorders and assessor's offices. The best internet sites use data from title companies as well as other sources to provide comprehensive data.

Finding the facts

Title companies, banks, credit unions, and online services such as RealtyTrac are all excellent resources for finding foreclosures. Each has a distinct level of information available to the end consumer.

Every time a homeowner is issued a notice of default, the notice is also sent to the title company. You can find all the title companies and all the notices of default; in fact many will even put you on a mailing list and email you the new NODs they receive each month or week. The notices give you the name of the person and their address, which is important when you send letters (send them personally) or call the individual. Make a list of all the title companies in your area, or select a few to start with. Start phoning them immediately. Ask to be transferred to someone who handles NODs. Most will be willing to work with you, but be forewarned that some will not. It does not hurt to throw them a bone; let them know you're interested in buying multiple properties and that you want a "partner" in the process. Usually what they provide is an emailed document, such as an Excel file, an Access database, or a PDF file. These are all excellent, and if your computer has the appropriate software you can add your own data and customize the files.

Since there are literally hundreds of title representatives in any geographic area, being able to find out the information is fairly simple to do. While every title company tends to have their own default services group, do not expect that department to be helpful at all. They merely receive all of the paperwork for the foreclosed properties, and lack any significant manpower to handle their day-to-day job, much less handle the hundreds, if not thousands of inquiries that they would get for actual properties. Rely on the title insurance agents, who stand to benefit if they receive the title policy for the transaction, as well as being able to assist in finding buyers for the property.

Banks and Credit Unions

Banks and credit unions (any lender, really) know when a property is at risk before anyone else. If you call any of the major banks, ask them who they use to report their NODs and their REOs. Typically, this will come from the banks' servicing group, unless they sell this information to a third party that manages the foreclosure process from beginning to end. In exchange for managing the process, these outside companies will charge a minimum fee, typically a percentage of the purchase price, which works counterproductive to your goal of wanting to save additional monies. Today they will often direct you to a web site or ask you to call back.

Getting information from them can be difficult; sometimes you need to start with a specific property you know that they own and go from there. Establish rapport with a banker or a lender that can help you. Note that 90 percent of the people that ask for these properties believe they will purchase a property for pennies on the dollar, which normally will just not happen. Time is valuable; many lenders such as Bill will guide you and counsel you if they believe you are serious. They want you to get a good deal, but they want you to do your homework, particularly the level of financial preparation and understanding of mortgage options we discuss in other chapters of this book.

Dani's husband worked with a lender to buy a property in Los Angeles County. He sold the property three years later for three times what he paid after putting about $90,000 into the home and living in it during its remodel.

Auctions

Auctions are usually held either at a courthouse or at an attorney's office. You must have cash or certified funds usually of at least $1,000 before you can bid, but check the specific auction details because this can vary *drastically*. All of the bidding in the auction is verbal, and the auctioneer will go through the list of homes at a very quick pace. You must listen to the legal description and the name of the debtor so you do not bid on the wrong property! Buying homes at these auctions can often result in a slight market discount, but it is better if you can buy in the pre-foreclosure stage or via a short sale in most cases.

High Bidder

If you are the high bidder, you will be asked to hand over your non-refundable deposit, which can be quite steep. You also must provide the trustee the entire purchase amount by a specified period of time, which is sometimes as short as 24 hours! Be prepared; have funding up front. If you have cash, this is easy; if you do not, you'll need to work with a bank that can provide immediate access to funds. This access should be lined up at least a week or two before attending the auction or you will not be prepared when you show up at the auction. Another option is to transfer money from a home equity line or even a credit card if you have the credit into your bank so you can provide a certified check, and then simply pay it off with a mortgage or by selling the home after you own it. If you need immediate cash, a hard-money lender will often front you the money you need to buy the home, but this will be an expensive route to go. This lender puts a second or third mortgage on the property, assuming that they can also place a lien against your primary residence. When you sell, the hard-money lender is paid off; definitely worth doing as an advanced investor but expensive. There are certainly better ways.

Be Prepared

Remember that at the auction, there is no title insurance available! You need to know absolutely everything about the property before you bid, so do your homework and be prepared. Know the fair market value, the home's condition, and what you expect to need to put in for repairs. Know what liens are on the home and understand completely what you're getting into. Be prepared for last minute filings by creditors so check the property out again (title) a couple of hours before the auction if you can with the title company. You may have to buy the home without inspecting the inside; if that is the case, assume the worst-case scenario. Any notes and liens that are ahead of the note in default (not in a subordinate position) remain on the property and they will be transferred to *you*, so do your homework if you go the auction route! We cannot stress this or over-emphasize it enough. Always, always, always pay the mortgages off through escrow so you know you're getting the deed; do not simply use a quitclaim deed (a transfer of interest in the property) to transfer the property. Word from the wise: Cut this corner, and you will be sorry in the long run. This is an unnecessary risk that some people promote in order to save a couple of thousand dollars. It is not worth cutting corners. Entrepreneurs are smarter than that!

Remember to register ahead of time. If you wait to register at the site, you may find a long line. The auction company says that the auctioneer wants all bidders to participate, so long lines will not mean that you will not get in—you will get your bidder number. If you are buying for your business, come with the Federal ID number at the time of your registration. You can register on behalf of someone else but you will need his or her full name, address, and documentation showing you have authority to execute documents on the individual's behalf.

> **Author's Note**
>
> In many states, documentation showing you have authority to execute documents on another individual's behalf is just a specific power of attorney. You can call your own attorney to have one drawn and verify this is all that is needed.

The bidder registration number the auction house assigns you shows you're an eligible buyer, so hang onto it. Ask for the order in which properties will be offered when you register and if there are any additions or deletions from the sale or updated information about the properties.

Try to have fun, be relaxed, and know what you are willing to pay. Seating is on a first come, first served basis; try to get there early so you can get a clear view of the screens on which the property photos and catalog numbers will be displayed for properties (Hudson and Marshall, 2007). Announcements at the auction take precedence "over written material." This is how the auctioneer corrects, updates, adds, or deletes information before bidding starts.

The Bidding Process

Introduce yourself to one of the bidding assistants, known as the "ring person," who is working the section of seating you are sitting in. Their job is to assist you during the auction by relaying bids to the auctioneer and answering your questions. Tell the bidding assistant which properties you are interested in and give them an opening bid:

> "...not your top price, but a reasonable start. When that property comes up for auction, the assistant will look to you for your bids. Several people may be bidding at first, but as the price increases, most will drop out. Each time a bid is recognized from another person you must decide whether or not to continue bidding. If your answer is yes, hold your bid number card or your hand in the air. Do not hesitate to call out to the bid assistant or to the auctioneer if you do not think they have noticed you. Make your decisions obvious." (Hudson and Marshall, 2007)

Local Auctions

There are local auctions for most major cities and towns. For instance, you can find local auctions for New York at www.biggerpockets.com/foreclosure-sales/newyork.html and Maryland at www.biggerpockets.com/ foreclosure-sales/maryland.html. You can also do an internet search for "local house home auction [state]" or "local house home auction [city]" inserting in the brackets the city and state that you're interested in. Often, this will result in home auction houses for that particular area that you can contact directly or online.

Online Sites

Another way to find auctions and even bid online is through online auction sites. Sites like RealtyTrac and others let you actually see live auctions and even bid online, or contact the broker that is handling bidding. Often, you have to put down a small amount of money ($2500 or less) for the individual to bid for you, and

Internet research provides for the most up-to-date information available in researching foreclosures. While you may be the exception to the rule, in general utilizing the newspaper will cause much more grief and stress than any expected level of success.

that money is then applied towards the down payment. These auctions usually give you 30 days to pay, which is great and more than enough time to get a loan—providing you've already done your homework.

Online Preparation

Hudson & Marshall is considered America's "premier" auction authority. You can read more about them at www.hudsonandmarshall.com. On their web site, you can view the available homes and even bid. Use their auction calendar or email info@hudsonandmarshall.com or phone 800-441-9401. You may want to attend an open house or schedule a showing by appointment with the broker in charge of the property. All auctioned real estate is as-is where-is, which means that whatever you see is what you're buying. Decide what the property is worth to you and come buy the property at the price you set. Try not to get involved in the "auction mentality." We suggest you come into the process in a manner that is similar to "sniping" an auction on eBay—put in your bid and if you get it, you get it. If you do not, do not worry about it and move on. Do your homework! Follow the instructions for H&M bidders (available on their web site or by phone).

The authors do find Hudson and Marshall's online search is a little cumbersome. It appears as though if you do not know a city or zip code with auctioned homes in it, you cannot find anything. But we found out (by playing with the system) that if you just enter nothing in the dialogue box, it will show you every home available currently for auction. Once you click on a property, you could map it and get information about where the auction is being held.

We recommend putting the information into comps sites to get an idea for what others on the block are selling for. One great one to use is www.domania.com, as it straight comps, rather than Zillow, which tries to estimate current value and may overestimate!

For instance, we looked at a home on 9622 Coastal Point Drive in Villa Rica, Georgia. Its zip code is 30180; the home is 2410 square feet and has four bedrooms and three baths. The photos of the home looked good. The system showed the last high bid of $222,000, so we immediately knew the next bidding price. One tip that we use from eBay: why bid yourself up? Wait until the last day to bid, even the last few minutes. If you enter your bid early, you're really bidding against yourself. This is the idea behind tools like Auction Snipers for eBay and the same rule should apply here.

Comparables in Domania showed between $214,000 and $280,000. The small map in Domania showed the property to be on or near a golf course or country club, and near a lake. To compare and show you what other systems value it at, Zillow valued it at $279,000, very close to the highest comp in Domania. If the home sells for near $222,000 and does not need heavy repairs, it may well be a very good deal. Zillow showed others on the street selling for well over $300,000 and the area appeared very nice online. If you cannot make it out there to see the property, try to contact the broker noted and see if he or she can send pictures to you and assess the property for you, or if you can have that individual meet a home inspector there before you bid.

Buying Homes Not Sold at Auction

Remember, sometimes a house will not sell at auction. This may be a good time to contact the lender and try to buy the home directly. This is called a "third bargain purchase opportunity." It does not necessarily mean the house is trashed, either. Consider mailing an overnight letter to the president of the bank with your offer and a letter of explanation about the foreclosed upon property that "didn't even sell at auction." You may want to enclose an earnest money deposit check to show sincerity. The letters rarely reach the president, of course, but a check will almost guarantee that they will reach the right department. While this process is somewhat random in its success, the potential for savings is gigantic if you exercise some patience in the search process. A client of one of my oldest friendships in real estate recently purchased a property for $148,000 that appraised for $450,000, by purposely searching for homes that did not sell at auction.

You will want to buy the property before it is listed with a real estate agent, so be sure to jump on this right away. These properties are few and far between, but they represent a magnificent investment opportunity. If the property is in awful condition, a picture or two showing just how bad it is might help, discouraging the lender from placing it on the market and incurring broker or agent fees.

Networking and Other Professionals

Purchase money escrow officers see the initial stages of foreclosure activity when the client attempts to combine mortgage payments during an initial refinance. These officers are responsible for handling payoff demands, along with all of the financial criteria for the handling of the loan, so they serve as an excellent resource in uncovering opportunities months in advance. These individuals' positions are designed to be completely neutral, but serve as the eyes and ears for a sophisticated lender or investor that is looking for opportunities before they reach market.

Real estate agents are often local real estate experts and know the particular area in which they work very well. But not all agents are created equal. Look for an agent with several years of experience, as many only know how to manage the busy markets, not the down or soft markets. A specific agent that comes to mind has been in the business for over 25 years; his business is increasing exponentially as the banks know he is very committed to the foreclosure and short sale markets, and can be counted upon to appropriately care for and market the listings provided by the bank. While they may not share it with lots of their clients, if you establish a relationship with an agent—particularly one that deals with foreclosures—you have a good chance of making an offer through an agent.

A listing agent (the agent that is selling the property) typically knows about six months in advance of a borrower heading down the foreclosure path. If you can get to know these agents, explain what your search criteria are, and show you're qualified already for a loan, they'll often work with you. Often they are paid by the banks, but sometimes they do expect payment from you. Find this out as soon as you begin to work with them. More often than not, this will not occur. What will occur, however, is that you establish a relationship with a real estate agent.

Internet Research

As we've said several times, internet research is imperative in this marketplace. Information and data is moving at a faster rate of change than the average consumer or even most real estate agents can keep up. However, in a consumer-centric web model, often consumers and the online marketplace is the best way to find out about the area you are investing in. What are some things you will want to know?

- Is the job market is beginning to tank in the area you're buying investment property in?
- Have rental comps (comparative rentals in the area) dropped five percent in the last three months?
- Is a big supplier of jobs in an area moving their plant to another region? Perhaps you will want to reconsider where you buy.

The internet in its infancy was just data distributed by individuals or business. People put information out there for public consumption, and the public acted on it. Today, the consumers themselves are giving out information freely—and often it is just as accurate as or more accurate than other indicators, because it is supplied by people living in the area or working for the company.

Better yet, consider this scenario: what if you knew ahead of time that a major manufacturing company employing thousands of workers was moving to a small city? Wouldn't it be wise to consider investing there, given the increasing need for homes? It has always been said that "real estate is local," and this is a great example. While the rest of the housing market may not be so hot, particular areas for particular reasons may be great.

Automated valuation or appraisal tools are a great resource in determining the appropriate value for potential investments. Know that they are merely guidelines as they tend to overestimate value, just as much as they sometime underestimate value.

Finding the facts

There are lots of excellent sites to help you do your research on the internet. Here is a list of tools that we recommend you check out:

- Zillow (www.zillow.com)
- RealtyTrac (www.RealtyTrac.com)
- AOL Real Estate (realestate.aol.com)
- Experian (www.experian.com)
- Homegain.com (www.homegain.com)
- Homes.com (www.homes.com)
- Yahoo! Real Estate (realestate.yahoo.com)
- Prudential California Realty (www.prudentialcaliforniarealty.com)
- Google (www.google.com: look for 'easter eggs' keywords)
- Downey Savings (www.downeysavings.com/ffs/properties)
- The Wall Street Journal Real Estate Journal (www.therealestatejournal.com)
- Domania (www.domania.com)
- Default Research (www.defaultresearch.com)
- REO Source (www.reosource.com)
- House Values (www.housevalues.com)
- Wilshire Credit Corp (www.wfsg.com/realestate)

So You Want to Make Money in Foreclosures!

When you begin investing in the foreclosure market, it is tempting to take the first deals you find—if they're foreclosures, they must be good deals, right? Not necessarily. Many "motivated" sellers (real estate buzzword for "desperate") can present an equally attractive deal if you do not know what to look for. RealtyTrac.com's Foreclosure Information Library contains an article on "Five Tips for Buying a Foreclosure Property Below Market Value" written by the CEO Jim Saccacio, all essential to making money in the foreclosure market.

Online Foreclosure Searches

There are many web-based services out there to help you find foreclosures, but in our opinion, RealtyTrac is tops in the market. The web services give you the ability as an average investor to find foreclosure (and even pre-foreclosure) information quickly and reliably. In the past, this information was only available to real estate professionals and high-value investors but as it is done in many markets, the internet has leveled the playing field.

The difference with RealtyTrac is that they had the vision to generate a site with great value to consumers and investors alike.

As noted in the article, "Five Tips for Buying a Foreclosure Property Below Market Value," persistence and patience are both required if you want to find a deal. Saccacio's tips are:

1. *Learn about the different types of properties and the foreclosure process.* You are doing this by reading this book! You should also supplement your reading with internet sites and other expert's opinions. Remember, there are many stages at which you can buy a home. Saccacio notes that the "best savings can be made at the pre-foreclosure stage, where homeowners can avoid foreclosures and lenders can save the time and cost involved in going through the process." In addition, he notes that immediately prior to the auction date is another good time, when both parties may be most open to a last minute resolution. Keep this in mind as you begin to time your decisions and your purchases, as we presume that you will continue to buy once you've successfully closed your first foreclosure purchase.

2. *Pre-qualify yourself before discussing any deals with sellers or banks.* This means that you should be prepared at a bare minimum to provide income and/or asset information to a lender (who has been highly recommended to you), as well as have a clear understanding of your current credit situation. A five-minute conversation with a mortgage lender that is taking your word in issuing a pre-qualification is not worth the paper it is written on, as it is not a commitment to lend. You are in the best possible position if the seller knows that you are able to follow through with the deal. Talk to your lender, and go through the complete approval process.

Preparation is a critical step; when buying a foreclosure at any stage, you want to be prepared so as to not create an even greater issue with the seller or the banks as they will want to work with people who appear to be prepared, not just those looking for a quick buck.

3. *Remember that the buyer and seller usually each have their own (most often separate) representative.* Go into the transaction with someone in your corner; the individual may help you pick the best property and negotiate a great price. It may be helpful to work with someone who specializes in the foreclosure market. Interview at least three agents who have been in the business more than five years. Many newer agents will be upset by this recommendation, but too many real estate agents are general practitioners, not specialists. Think of your medical provider in this situation. Would you want a family medicine doctor to analyze the heart condition that runs in your family? Is your financial health that much less important?

4. *Do your homework.* Remember that any purchase made in the foreclosure market is generally considered riskier than in traditional buying and selling of real estate. The most important consideration in doing your homework is to understand that it takes time. If you expect to close a foreclosure or short sale deal to be completed in 30 days, without being completely prepared financially, you will be disappointed and frustrated. There are multiple parties involved who are all trying to protect their financial interests and this process simply takes a bit of time. If you can stick it out, you will be successful and end up with an incredible financial reward. You need to understand not only the property you are buying, along with the market you are buying it in, but also the entire process—and potential pitfalls, which we discuss in this book.

5. *Be realistic with your offer.* You do want a deal, but you do not want to low-ball a seller so severely that you risk the seller never considering any of your offers—ever! No one is going to give you the property for free, and if someone can easily get a higher price elsewhere they probably will. Also, as Saccacio points out in his article, remember that the sellers are often in distress and may be difficult to deal with, especially when they are just finding out their home is going to

be foreclosed upon. Make a realistic offer and know the property's value and what is owed on it. Remember that the value of the property today may be quite different in many markets than it was three to six months ago, so this is a critical area to address.

Scouting Pre-Foreclosures Online

Since pre-foreclosures often provide the best deal for the buyer, it is in your best interest to try to find pre-foreclosures before they become full-blown REOs. RealtyTrac's "Buying Pre-Foreclosures" section of their web site recommends considering the following things when searching for these foreclosures:

Find and File Properties

To find and file properties, you need up-to-date information on pre-foreclosures and you must act *fast*. This is one huge benefit the internet offers.

Be sure to get comparative analyses on properties you are considering. By typing the address into Zillow and other online appraisal tools, you can find out if the home is even remotely in the ballpark of the price you should be paying—and it will help you make a reasonable offer. Realize this is only a starting point in finding out an accurate value, which certainly does not replace the professional opinion of an appraiser.

There are organizations that offer you subscriptions to properties as they become available on a nationally updated database (we'll talk more about this in the final chapter).

"Filing" means developing a system of tracking properties you have interest in. Store files on these properties either in your local hard drive or an online site. If the property is in your local area, drive by it. If it isn't, get online and start searching for information on the area; use tools like Zillow and Google Earth to look at the specific area, street, and zip code.

Confirm the Status of the Home

Remember, once the home goes into pre-foreclosure, an owner has two to three months to try to reinstate the loan. Reinstatement stops the foreclosure process. This is one reason it is important to have numerous homes in your file—they can disappear from the foreclosure listings if the owner makes arrangements with the lender. Call the trustee or attorney assigned to the property to see if it has been reinstated. You will need access to the trustee information, again available online. Most of the time you will not find out anything besides whether the home is still in the foreclosure process or not, but this is all you need to know for now.

> **Author's Notes**
>
> Trustees and attorneys are used to receiving calls from buyers interested in foreclosure properties. The first few may feel awkward, but that is normal. In time, you will become more comfortable with the notion that you did not cause the individual who defaulted to go into foreclosure, and you are operating in an ethical and legal manner. If you are really interested in a property, stay on top of it!

Confirm the Value

Find out as much information as you possibly can about the estimated market value of the home, how much is owed on the home, and if the owner has other liens (builder liens, taxes, etc.) against the property that will need to be paid off (therefore requiring the owner to get a higher value to settle). This information is all public. Go to the county recorder's office, many of which now offer the information online. You can also use online tools through service providers to help.

Be sure not to let this process take more than a day or two because chances are, you aren't the only one watching the property. In addition to comparable sales figures (i.e., what similar properties in the area have recently sold for, referred to as "comps"), look at the date the property was purchased and the loan balances. When looking at comparable value, you should first take into account *closed* sales as they are the best determinant factor, then pending sales that are in escrow, and last but certainly not least, listings that merely indicate what the seller would like to sell for before any negotiations. Take the estimated market value of the home, minus any potential need for repairs, minus any liens or balances, to determine the home's potential. Again, your goal here is to determine what it will take to help the seller break even—where they will neither benefit nor gain from the sale of the home—or at the very least feel like the transaction is a win-win, assuming they have some equity built in that they hope to hold on to.

Contact the Owner

This step is often hardest for individuals, especially if you feel badly for the seller of the home. While we believe that you should be empathetic about the situation, when you contact the owner, you must keep in the back of your mind that this is a business decision for both of you. You can make this call yourself, or you can hire a real estate agent on your behalf if you really do not have the time to make the call yourself. Usually, though, the owner will be less intimidated by an understanding potential buyer than some agent calling (which by the way, they probably are experiencing every day).

Whether personally or otherwise, express your interest in the property to the owner. Sometimes it is best if you do it yourself because the seller hears a real person behind the call and may not feel frustrated by the forced sale of their home being considered from a business perspective. Before you spend any time on this, be sure you are completely prepared to buy the home, and make sure you are qualified to do so.

If the owner has listed the property, then just call the listing agent. However, note that once it is listed, there is less bargaining potential in general and the seller is being advised by a real estate agent that wants the home to sell, but also wants to maximize the profit for themselves. Remember that the owner only has a limited amount of time, as they are on a timetable as well. To check to see if the property is listed, use any of the MLS services available online, including www.realestateagent.com or the tools in the actual system you use to find your foreclosures.

Usually, the owner will not have the home listed. Be proactive here and contact them. When you cut out the agent's commissions of 5 to 7 percent, not only is your chance for a lower price greater (since the seller pays the commissions to the agent) but again, you are also putting a name and a "human touch" behind the offer. Sadly, though sometimes deservedly, real estate agents have a "shady" reputation in line with attorneys, used car salesmen, and mortgage brokers (ah, such great company we keep!).

You may wish to contact the owner by mail. However, we assure you that the owner is receiving lots of letters from real estate agents, investors, scam artists, collection departments, to name a few, all looking for an angle to work with the owner. Personal experience in this arena shows that these letters are rarely followed up on with a simple telephone call, which greatly improves your ability to get through to the owner. Be sure that you mention in your written correspondence, as well as your phone call, that you want it to work for both parties. We suggest you *not* mention the word foreclosure—it is a touchy subject and is a sure way to alienate the seller since it can be quite embarrassing to the owner or anyone who sees the letter.

Remember that the owner has some time, often many months, between the initial foreclosure notice and a public auction. You may not receive responses right away, while the owner is considering all available opportunities, or sometimes denying that the situation is as bad as it appears. Owners often initially do not want to sell, as they feel that they are giving up their dream of home ownership. What you hope is they come to realize that selling is better than losing the property through a foreclosure auction. For this reason, you may need to send several follow-up postcards or letters before you find anyone who is truly interested, or even send multiple postcards or letters to the same owner if you are really interested in a specific property. As the auction date approaches, the owner has more incentive to call you.

> A recent client of Bill's had been working on a property and had called the owner several times over the course of six months. Thirty days prior to the sale, the owner realized all of the other interested parties were no longer available—and the one person who they remembered genuinely wanted to help called them once again. Ultimately, the client was able to secure a significant equity position of $450,000 on a $1.4 million property that was scheduled to go to auction by bringing the payments current and purchasing the property within a week of the auction date.

As the RealtyTrac article points out, be prepared for a rude response from owners, as these methods are sometimes inherently confrontational.

Although some may get impatient with this approach, some investors find this to be the best course because it immediately rules out anyone not interested in selling. Remember, however, that even in this pre-foreclosure stage, the owner has rights. If the owner does not want to consider your offer, do not push it. If the owner does not respond to any inquiry, you may still be able to buy the house or land at a public auction. The auction occurs only if the owner does not sell the property or pay off the amount owed. You can call the trustees or attorneys appointed for the property to find out the status of a specific property.

In-Person Meeting

At any stage in the foreclosure timeline, if you are able to negotiate a purchase price, meet with the owners to talk about the property. Walk through the property and be prepared to buy it "as is." Keep an eye out for estimated repairs, but note that the more of a "fixer upper" the home is, the more upside financial potential there generally is if you're willing (and can afford) to put work into the home.

Equity Splits

Sometimes the loan that is in default is what is called "assumable" and you may be able to pay off the amount in default and simply take over payments. If not, you have to pay off the full loan amount and any other liens on the property. If the owner has equity in the property after the mortgage and any liens, you may ask the owner split the equity with you. This lets you retain cash, and acquire a property below its value. This is referred to as an equity "split." Despite the name, this does not necessarily (in fact, usually does not) mean a 50/50 split; it is one you find fair given your work and "bailing out" of the owner, and the owner finds acceptable as well. This can often be a sticking point, so go in with an open mind and your bottom line number in your head.

Finding the facts

Equity splits are a great win-win opportunity for the current owner and the buyer to strike a deal that benefits both parties. This is one of many ways to share the equity with the current homeowner.

Owner Goodwill Can Earn You Money

If you are willing to be creative in helping owners out of their financial distress, they may be more willing to work with you. On RealtyTrac's web site, they suggest perhaps offering to let the owner stay in the home for a certain period of time (while even possibly paying you rent) until they find a new home. You may offer to pay their housing costs for the first month or more after they leave. You may let them stay and pay rent until you decide to resell the house if it is an investment property. Try to understand the needs of the specific owner. Ask lots of questions and find a way that you can help them. Showing genuine concern and really going out of your way will give you an edge over others who may be trying to buy, and will instill a sense of trust rather than resentment towards you for being able to afford a home that they lost.

Contact With Lender

During the negotiation of the purchase agreement, contact the foreclosing lender and any lien holders. Let them know you plan to buy the property and intend to take care of all liens (RealtyTrac, 2006). You may even be able to negotiate a lower pay-off amount. You are, after all, saving the bank the trouble of trying to sell the home, paying a broker, and sending the home to auction. Sometimes the lenders and lien holders do clear liens for less than the amount owed, particularly when the lenders and lien holders are aware of your knowledge, experience, financial preparation, and desire to work with them. Remember, people work with people they like. The employees, who work in every stage of the foreclosure process, naturally gravitate towards those individuals that make their jobs easier.

RealtyTrac suggests that the goal as a buyer is to purchase a property, including paying all liens and repairs, for at least 20 to 30 percent below full market value, although it is possible to get better deals—and both authors have seen them! And in addition, we've only seen the beginning of this current trend. As long as sellers continue to utilize their properties as if they are bottomless piggy banks without understanding the impact of their financing decisions in conjunction with changing market demand, their personal purchasing power will continue to deteriorate, affecting their ability (or inability) to pay, causing more opportunities for buyers and investors alike. While we are currently within historical numbers of bank-owned properties, the number of foreclosure filings is increasing exponentially that, with the use of the internet, are exposed far sooner than ever before, allowing a much better opportunity at purchasing a property at a substantial discount—to those who prepare.

Once you and the owner have an agreement and you've contacted all lien holders and mortgagees, put the agreement in writing. You need to write up a purchase agreement. You can have a real estate agent or a real estate attorney do this, or in certain escrow states, have the escrow instructions serve as a joint purchase agreement. You may download forms and do it yourself, but it isn't recommended. Be sure that the deal is contingent on a full title search conducted by a licensed title company or attorney, and contingent on a property inspection. You want to know if the roof is about to fall in, as that can quickly eat into your 20 to 30 percent savings! Remember, however, that contingencies expire. You will need to act quickly—get the title search done quickly and do your inspection within a few days to avoid any surprises and keep yourself out of any potential trouble with canceling a deal if you need to.

So, what about your ability to actually buy the home? We'll address that next.

Credit Scoring and Assets

We talked in earlier chapters about what your credit score means, but we need to touch on assets, liquid or otherwise, and how they are tied in with your credit score and profile. It is preferable that you have a combination of liquid assets, as well as equity that can be used for investment purposes. We are big believers in leveraging equity as long as you have the financial ability to handle the increases in payments as a result of higher equity line rates, fully amortizing loans, decreases in market value, or any combination thereof.

If you have assets that have equity, it may be easier to qualify for these foreclosure loans if the bank sees that you can effectively manage debt while using your equity intelligently. Again, the bank does not want to compound their mistakes by loaning new money to a borrower who at some time in the future may default as well, ending up in foreclosure yet again. In this regard, one of Bill's neighbors is an aggressive investor, who understands how to leverage her earnings, credit, and more importantly, the equity in her properties to purchase additional properties. She understands cash flow better than most people, realizing that in most areas throughout the U.S., you will need to place a significant down payment on a property in order to generate income each month, rather than having a negative cash flow on a monthly basis.

You may read other books, listen to programs, or even watch infomercials on late night television that illustrate how to build a real estate portfolio without any of your own money, but that speaks to the contrary. From the investor and banker's perspectives, we can assure you that this approach is the exception rather than the rule. One person out of a thousand may be able to make their system work if all of the planets and moons are properly aligned. Conversely, we suggest that you start from ground zero with a firm understanding of your individual financial standing, tolerance for risk, as well as knowing how and where to start. Avoid videos or DVDs that are heavy on promises but light on the steps necessary to create wealth through real estate foreclosures.

As you've learned, you need to move quickly on foreclosure deals, so be sure to have your assets readily available in a binder, or online in an easily accessible PDF file, as well as having a real estate summary that clearly identifies cash flow from other properties in an easy to understand spreadsheet. It pays to keep this schedule current, particularly in the area of rents! Again, a reputable lender can spot if the rents you are charging for current properties are in line with the area, or if you have room to renegotiate rents in anticipation of purchasing additional foreclosure properties. Technology allows us to review our current portfolios, a market area, a specific zip code, or even a specific tract to determine if the data we're receiving is accurate. Take a look at www.rentometer.com and you can quickly see what others are paying in rent by numerous search options.

The bottom line: Having your assets in order allows you to make a true determination of your ability to purchase multiple foreclosure properties in the coming months and years. You will thank yourself for being so organized—buying multiple properties is a lot easier with the right level of preparation.

Improvements and Do-It-Yourself (DIY) Projects

Many people buy foreclosures and assume that they'll be able to fix them up themselves. If you are in the building trades or just good with your hands, this type of project may become a worthwhile endeavor, as you'll understand the true cost of repairing a property before you own it. If for some reason you are not in an industry or capacity that is directly related to the home improvement industry, add 10 to 20 percent over and above your anticipated costs to hire professionals, as there are several things that could cause significant cost over-runs. Padding costs is absolutely essential; expect the worst and hope for the best.

Also, be aware of the fact that if you buy a hard-core fixer-upper, it may take months to get it ready for resale or rent. This means that you will be paying the mortgage and interest this entire time, not to mention taxes and insurance. You have to calculate all of this into the equation when you make your initial offer. The absolute worst-case scenario is to buy the home and have to take months or even years to make it resalable, and have numerous surprise issues come up with the home. This can easily eat away part of or even your entire equity position!

If you are good with improvements and have time to dedicate to it, we're all for doing it yourself and saving money. Just make sure you balance the money you save with the mortgage you have to pay! You do not want to save $5,000 in labor costs and extend the project by six months, paying $7,000 in additional mortgage fees, plus six extra months of no rental income, compounded by the additional investment of your time that is rarely accounted for! The numbers simply do not add up if you do not approach do-it-yourself projects with a high level of knowledge. Again, when purchasing foreclosure properties, it is critical that you look at both best-case and worst-case scenarios. It will make a huge difference.

Research and Preparation

When Dani bought her first investment property, the real estate agent she worked with told her she must be ready to sign documents in two hours; meaning from the time he phoned her until the time she had to sign, she had two hours to do research. It was in the heat of the

If a deal presented itself tomorrow, would you be prepared to move forward with it? If the answer is no, you should do everything in your power to get your financial house in order within the next 30 days so you're aware of where your credit and assets stand, to be able to start buying and investing.

market and numerous offers and backup offers were being submitted on one property.

Today's market isn't quite as heated, so you have a little (albeit *a little)* more time to do homework up front. Do not waste time, but do not be foolish, either. Be sure you've done your homework, you are prepared, you are pre-qualified if you aren't using cash, you have your equity line or funds ready if you are. Simply have everything ready ahead of time so you know if the deal you are looking for presents itself, you will be ready to close.

Why is this so important? With the cooling housing market, it isn't such a big deal; in fact, people take their time intentionally to get better prices, waiting for sellers to become frustrated. But, with foreclosures, the prices are usually so hot that it mimics a very hot real estate market—only even more intense. You must move quickly and cannot delay in closing, as foreclosure banks tend to have even less tolerance than a normal seller. If you appear unprepared, unmotivated, or simply unable to handle the transaction, the bank will move on, as they simply have not been prepared for the onslaught of properties coming back to them as foreclosures and short sales in a relatively short period of time. If it is truly a good purchase, there will be prepared buyers waiting in line.

As mentioned previously, we are within historical numbers as foreclosures are a norm in the real estate industry; what is different today is that the speed at which they are coming back to the banks is a direct correlation to the relaxed lending standards combined with the low credit scores and lack of assets on the borrowers behalf. You need to be ready to sign a deal tomorrow if that is what was required. You need to be mentally prepared to talk to buyers, and you need to be prepared to take a bit of risk. Just how much risk will most often be associated with the bargain you get and potential money you stand to earn; however, you can certainly take lower risk deals that do not have as great of equity positions.

One difficult thing to overcome is the mental preparation. People are used to having time to review their options when making big decisions; when individuals or families decide to move into a bigger (or smaller home), change areas, or a job change forces a move. There is usually time to think, time to research, and time to react. In a foreclosure market, you have time to research areas (before you find properties) but once a specific property is found, there's not much time to act on it. Getting yourself into the mindset of acting quickly and being unafraid of what's to come is a good thing to start doing now. Money, or access to capital, provides for great comfort. You should be comfortable with any decision that is made, once you've gathered your data, thought it through, and are prepared to move forward.

You will also need to be sure you have proof of funds for your down payment and/or any reserve requirements ready. If you are looking at properties of one to four units, you'll need to consider down payments of 10 percent or greater and additional reserve requirements available of a minimum three months to six months. Properties over four units will become commercial financing most of the time, which increases the down payment requirements, increases the interest rate, and decreases your overall financial flexibility as the more creative financing terms are off the table on commercial properties. You'll want to know how good of a deal you're willing to take—what discount to market value? Will you be holding onto these properties for a couple of years, or just a couple of months? Given the answers, are you being realistic that the property will be worth what you think it will be worth during these predetermined time frames? Will you accept a 10 percent discount to market value in exchange for lower risk? Are you comfortable receiving a 20 percent discount although it carries greater risk? How about a 30 percent discount to value, or 50 percent without even having an inspection, in another county or another state? Assess this early.

Other questions to answer ahead of time include: How will you pay the mortgage on it once it is closed? Are you borrowing the money to make this happen? Does your payment include the tax and insurance payments, or is this something you intend to pay later? Will the tenants move in immediately, as they promised they would? What if you can't flip it as quickly as you thought, if the property needs more work than you anticipated, or the rental market is tight? What are your plans—and perhaps more importantly, your contingency plans? Who will you work with? What are you trying to accomplish? How will you plan for the time required to fix up the home? Will you list it on your own or with an agent? Would using an agent cost you money or save you money?

Once you can answer these questions, at a bare minimum, then you are ready to begin the process of *finding* a home or multiple homes as foreclosure purchases or short-sale transactions. Let us give you some advice; if you have time on your hands, do it yourself, otherwise hire a professional to do the sifting for you.

Valuing Your Gem

We've discussed appraisals in regard to the impact they have on getting a loan. Let's step back a minute and talk about the need to be able to get an accurate appraisal of the value of a property you are considering. While valuing a home is an appraiser's job, you will need to understand not only the process, but even perhaps do some or all of the work yourself. First, let's take a look at what an appraiser does and what their normal procedures are. Remember, some of this you may end up doing yourself!

One thing we need to caution you about. While we are huge fans of tools like Zillow and automatic appraisal sites online, keep in mind that they're based on old information (previous closings), which may mean the property you are interested in could be worth substantially more or substantially less. Recent analyses have shown weakness in these appraisal sites as they use public record information that fails to recognize neighborhood boundaries, upgrades, and other items that can significantly impact the value of a home. It also means that while we love these sites for research purposes, we feel strongly that you should get an appraisal, and do a self walk-through as well as get the opinion of other experts, if there is time to do so. There may not be, and so you will need to rely on your lender (if you're using one) for fast turnaround times on valuation or on online tools. We've found Domania to be quite accurate for an online user-based (i.e., non professional) tool.

The Vitals

There are some vital pieces of information you will need to know, such as the square footage of the home, the size of the lot, the number of bedrooms, the number of bathrooms, and the year the home was built. These are the fundamentals that are relevant and important and they will be critical to doing a comparative analysis. Even tools online like Zillow and RealtyTrac will show you "comps" with most of this information so you'll need to have something to compare your potential home to. If a property appears to be overvalued, or undervalued, there may be an error as it relates to the correct square footage, capital improvements such as pools and spas, or even unpermitted or modified structures that are not included in the valuation tools' criteria search. Remember, too, that any additions may increase your property tax assessment if square footage is increased.

True Comps

Part of finding comparable properties or "comps" is to research recent sales in the same neighborhood. Usually, we recommend homes within one mile because neighborhoods can differ so drastically outside of that range. If possible, choose the same home tract, because home prices can be drastically different in sub divisions one mile apart. If you can find a home in the same tract and within half a mile, that is even better. Appraisers will have to find at least three similar-sized homes that have sold and *closed escrow*, which means that the deal is recorded and the new owner has taken possession and recorded the deed in the same neighborhood. Most appraisers require the home to be within one mile and have sold within the past six months. Sometimes, you can get a lender to bend a few of these rules if you can show that the homes on the market are going for substantially more than a home that closed six months ago, or if the most recent comp is 5-6 months old and you can show solid appreciation in that comp's value. The further that you move away from the subject property, the harder you are making it on the appraiser to be effective in regards to value, unless there are highly specific factors allowing for this to occur. Case in point: a builder one of the authors is working with on a semi-custom project believes that his quality is so far superior to anything else in the area that he is willing to look up to ten miles to support his view. Ironically, none of the appraisers support his view, yet he is bent on convincing all of the professionals that he is right, and they are wrong. Can you say "out of touch with reality"?

The Comp Process

Appraisers will go to the home and look at not only the property, but also the exterior of the comparable homes to estimate values. Usually, the appraiser (and you'll want to do the same) will take photos of the curb appeal (street side of the home), the rear of the home, the view up and down the street (remember that the curb appeal isn't only of your home but of all the homes around it), and then the appraiser will often inspect the interior of the home. The appraiser does *not* do an inspection of the home's structure. The appraiser is only looking for items that would add to or take away from the *value* of the home. Remember the value is determined by the marketplace, whether buyer and seller agree, along with having the support of the marketplace through comparable analysis.

Spend a few hundred dollars on appraisals and inspections to make sure you are making a worthy investment. This will save you THOUSANDS in the long run.

When you do your own walk-thru (assuming you are given the opportunity) be thorough and look for both—but by all means, certainly hire a professional inspector too.

Appraisers will draw the floor plan of the home and often measure each room to do so. Sometimes, the appraisers can pull plans or use previous appraisals done on the property to save time. Remember that the other homes, the comps, are only inspected on the exterior. You can pull data from the Multiple Listing Service (MLS), county and public records, and previous appraisal files to determine the inside amenities of the comparable homes; a good appraiser will take this into consideration. If your neighbor has an identical home and the homes are relatively similar on the outside, sometimes the inside (a kitchen remodel for instance) will be a distinguishing factor and compared with the neighbor (assuming they were both on the market at the same time) yours should sell quicker and/or for a higher price.

The Final Analysis

Sometimes slight adjustments can be made in the appraisal if you're unhappy or feel it is unfair, but remember that the appraiser in this particular case is helping you—you do not want to buy a home that you will not make money on. If the appraiser comes in with a value on a foreclosure property way under what you estimated, go with it. Chances are the appraiser knows something about the area and the condition of the home that you may not, and it isn't worth the risk. Move on. Also, remember that the neighborhood and what the neighborhood looks like *does* play a factor in the final value of the home! Some estimates suggest that over 90 percent of the time, the condition of the exterior of the home is almost identical to the interior. As a homeowner, savvy people will increase the curb appeal of the home to make the appraiser think the inside is comparable. Since this is an often-applied technique, be sure to have the appraiser go inside or do it yourself. Some of this information was suggested in the article "Understanding Appraisals" at www.mortgageunderwriters.com/understand.html, which we highly recommend you read for more information.

More Tips and Tricks to Finding Great Foreclosures

There are lots of people who know about foreclosures before the general public is made aware of them. For instance, many foreclosures occur because a couple divorces and neither wants to cover the mortgage, or out of spite one refuses to for various reasons, including to destroy the other's credit. Divorce attorneys therefore often know of foreclosures early. Since the attorney cannot break client confidentiality, you will need to find one that has clients who want people to be aware of their home for sale before it hits foreclosure or before one or the other individual files for bankruptcy. Consequently, bankruptcy attorneys also often know of potential foreclosures because they know if the person or couple is at risk for default.

Financial Planners (again confidentiality is a potential problem) have great access to pre-foreclosures and many have clients that want their planners to tell others to save them from the entire foreclosure process. If any of these individuals are within your sphere of influence, have a discussion with them to see if they will even present the idea to their clients in the

> The financials are far more important than the home itself; if you cannot afford the home, it does not matter how much you love it. Think rationally and logically, not emotionally when investing in foreclosures.

Finding the facts

off chance that one of their clients is faced with this type of difficult situation. They may or may not wish to discuss this with their clients for fear of getting too close to what can be a highly charged emotional situation. You are not discussing the client with them; they will take care of these themselves. You merely want access to the situation if it should present itself.

Buying a HUD Home

A Housing and Urban Development (HUD) home is a one- to four-unit (yes, you can buy multi-unit properties) residential property acquired by this government agency as a result of a foreclosure auction on an FHA-insured mortgage, discussed earlier in the book. HUD becomes the property owner and offers it for sale to recover the loss on the foreclosure claim. HUD has their own web site at www.hud.gov. Almost anybody can buy a HUD home. If you have cash or you qualify for a loan (with some restrictions), you may buy a HUD home. HUD homes are offered to owner-occupant purchasers (people buying the homes to live in) before they are offered to investors. You can search properties at www.hud.gov/homes/index.cfm. Any unsold property following the "priority period for owner occupants" is then available to everyone, including investors. All homes offered for sale are listed on the internet by management companies that HUD contracts with. Each market area will have a specific agency or broker to handle this business exclusively. Any real estate broker registered with HUD may submit an offer and contract to purchase on your behalf. The best part yet? HUD pays the real estate broker's commission, if it is included in the contract.

There are some designated areas around the country that are available at reduced prices to police officers, teachers, firefighters, emergency medical technicians (EMTs), and employees of non-profits and local governments under the Good Neighbor Initiative. The philosophy behind this is two fold—first, it is believed that communities thrive when these individuals or groups live in the area where they work; second, while each of these groups earns a respectable annual income, it takes a few years or longer to achieve it, during which time that many people leave these industries as they cannot make a "comfortable living." HUD helps encourage them to stay in the profession with a little relief on their housing costs. The discount can be as steep as fifty percent off for homes in revitalized areas. HUD will require you sign a second mortgage and note for the discount amount, and no payments are required on the "silent amount" provided you fulfill the three-year occupancy rule, meaning that you will live in the home for three years. You can combine HUD homes, even discounted HUD homes, with FHA loans if you're going to live in the home, since FHA does not do investor financing.

Even if you are buying a HUD home (some would say especially if you are), you should get an inspection and you have an inspection period after your offer is accepted. All HUD homes are sold as-is and have no warranty, and HUD (unlike banks) will not give you any credit or make repairs for any problem whatsoever, so do not even try negotiating this. They also do not offer direct financing, so you'll want to find a lender to help you. The table below shows you what a listing looks like. Information has been modified to protect the privacy of the individual. As you can see, the escrow amount is shown, and the status is still in the "occupant priority" phase. If

Property [Parcel Number]	Details	
[Photo Here]	Address:	[Street, City, State, Zip, County]
	Price:	$355,000
	As-Is Value:	$355,000
	Appraisal Date:	10/17/2004
	Bed/Bath:	4/2
	Sqft:	1,956
	Year:	1999
	FHA Financing:	Insured with Repair Escrow (IE)
	203K Eligible:	No
	List Date:	12/22/2005
	Bid Deadline:	01/01/2006 at 13:59:59
	Priority:	Owner Occupant
	Property Condition:	Click here to view the Property Condition Report
	Status:	Property Available for Bidding (Owner Occupant Priority)
View Map	Escrow Amount:	$4,510

MORE INFORMATION:
Only HUD registered Brokers can place a bid. Click here to find a HUD registered broker in your area.

Special Comments

Property is being offered Owner Occupant only. Offers must be submitted by 11:59PM on 1/01/06 to be considered for the 1/02/06 bid opening. Property is listed FHA Insurable (IE) with the following escrow repairs—Cumulative structural repairs totaling $4,510. (Repairs consist of damages to subfloor, siding, roof, and other miscellaneous items.) Property Characteristics—Yr. Blt 1999; GLA—1956 sqft; Lot Size—Approx. 3.65 acres.

Retrieved from http://hud2.towerauction.net/CA.htm

you are an investor you'll need to check back. The special comments section offers very little information and shows which escrow repairs must be done and what year the home was built, as well as how large the lot is (huge for California!) While at the time we checked, HUD showed just one home in California, there were over 1200 in Texas, broken down by city or county. Have fun hunting for homes! There are some incredible deals out there, but you have to look hard and be persistent. HUD data tends to be accurate, as it is a government web site.

Special Issues In Financing Foreclosure Deals

There are certainly special circumstances and curve balls that can be thrown into foreclosure deals. Not only are they unusual, they sidestep the tried and true methods of purchasing homes. There are several potential issues to be aware of ahead of time.

Low Appraisal

Analyzing value is a key for anyone purchasing a foreclosure. We've mentioned this a few times, but the bank will really care about it! By the bank, we mean both the bank you're trying to short sell from (assuming you are) and the bank that is lending you the money. Both want to know they're getting a good deal.

One potential glitch in this process is if the home appraises significantly under the market value. The bank you are using to finance the property will not take kindly to this and since loans often have appraisal contingencies, a low appraisal may require you to put more cash down, find a new lender altogether, or not purchase the home at all. Foreclosure deals do not have time even for things like loan shopping and finding your W2s, let alone dealing with a low appraisal. Have everything ready, and make sure you do enough leg work that you

Finding the facts

Don't know if a deal is worth pursuing? You can get quick comps online but try to balance them with appraiser estimates. Sometimes comps online can be over-inflated and don't take into consideration local concerns such as freeway noise or an airport.

minimize the risk of a value issue. Find out ahead of time what specific number, or value, the bank you're using to finance the deal will want to make the deal happen, and find out precisely what will occur if the home does not hit that target. Will the lender pull the deal? Ask for more money down? Only raise your rate a bit? Know this ahead of time and be ready. Your success in this area will completely depend on your ability to anticipate the issues that may present themselves by planning ahead.

Contingencies

If you really like the home and the area, you may wish to make your deal not contingent on the appraisal and/or inspection. The reason we suggest this? Sellers know that you can get out of a deal if the property does not appraise and if the inspection fails. They also know that usually buyers use the inspection as a means to cut down their offer even more, based on all the "repairs the home needs." For example, Dani had a buyer give her an offer for a home in Texas, only to follow it up with a list of 40 things he wanted fixed (like light bulbs)—or $5,000 towards his closing costs! Obviously, that was his goal all along.

If you remove those contingencies, there is technically no reason the seller will not get their money, and the same holds true for the bank you're trying to buy from or short sell from. Quite simply, these non-contingent deals are just more attractive and if there are multiple people competing for a home, most agents would recommend the seller go with the non-contingent offer. However, this is really risky in a foreclosure situation unless you have seen the home, you know a lot of details about it, and you are certain it will not only appraise for its value (or darn close) but will not have any issues with it. At the end of the day, you will be paying for the difference between the purchase price and the appraised value if you agree to not have an appraisal contingency clause in the purchase agreement.

Worst-Case Scenario

Work a worst-case scenario on value, rents, and rate of appreciation. You have some numbers in your head (or perhaps on your spreadsheet—

we hope!); the amount you'd like to earn off of the deal, the amount you'd like to rent it for, the value versus the amount you are paying, etc. After all, if you didn't, you'd have no reason to go into the deal to begin with. However, you need to have a contingency plan. You need to have a worst-case scenario for each of these three things: value, rent and rate of appreciation.

Starting with value—if the appraisal comes in low, will you continue to go ahead with the purchase or nix the deal? Will you ask for a lower price and risk losing it with the seller? This will be weighed, of course, with the rate of appreciation you expect, and perhaps the rent or cash flow you expect the property to have. But, what if the rental comps do not come in at the number you expect? What if you cannot cover the mortgage on the place? Is it still worth it? What if the area hit a 12 percent gain last year, but this year only hits 5 percent? Still worth it? Worst case—what if all three happen?

A Worst Case Example

Dani purchased two homes in Bullhead City, Arizona, and then built two more—right in the middle of the peak of the real estate boom in 2005 and early 2006. Shortly after, the area, which is highly dependent on Californians taking out equity lines to buy second homes, tanked. Californians couldn't get appraisals for the value they needed, or were too afraid of the market to go buying new homes. These spec houses that she built were expected to make a minimum of $50,000 each in profit, based on comps at the time she signed the deals. After they were done, and after paying about $12,000 in construction interest during the build-out for each one out of her monthly paycheck, Dani had one on the market for two years, and the other for a year. No buyers—not even an offer. She lowered the price several times. Finally, she decided to rent them—now owing $20,000 less than they were worth on each one, and having paid out over $40,000 in interest. She found a renter for one—a renter that refused to let her sell it while she was living in it! The other is still on the market at the time of this book writing, and has been for over a year. Not only did the appreciation take a hit, the value took a hit and in fact went negative, and the rents took a hit.

Dani learned a worst-case scenario lesson that you can learn from without the pain of going through it; her contingency plan was to rent, but the rental market fell flat, too. Her backup plan was to use stocks to pay for the mortgages, again foregoing potential gains. This is precisely why lenders put interest rate penalties on investors. If she didn't have the money to cover all her properties, she would have paid her primary mortgage before these homes. It is a perfect example of why you must assume all three worst-case scenarios will happen at the same time, and then figure out how you will handle it—all before you buy!

How Fast Can the Bank Close the Deal?

So you make a deal with a seller, you call the bank with your authorization to release and convey information, agreeing to purchase a short sale of the property. Now you are dependent on an extremely fast transaction with your lender, presuming they have approved the deal in advance; speed is of the essence. If you can close in 14-21 days, your offer will have a greater propensity for acceptance because you will be writing this into the original offer. This is called the escrow period, and it is usually 30 days because it takes this long to order appraisals, to get documentation, inspections, etc., and then to fund loans. How-

> Bill uses e-mail aggressively to communicate and inform in a way that clearly outlines the next step to each borrower. On several occasions, he has sent e-mails between 1:00 and 4:00 am, as the commitment was made to the borrower that they would have the information first thing in the morning so they would have an opportunity to communicate with the bank.

ever, banks can and do act faster and you may want to find yourself one. Most lenders will promise they can deliver, but very few actually will. You will usually know by how quickly they return your initial call, as well as the manner in which they communicate. Lender software has become advanced enough that most disclosures and documents can be sent via e-mail directly to the borrower.

If you can close in two to three weeks, you stand a greater chance for things going wrong on the lending side if you are not prepared, though you will stand a greater chance of the owner and the bank accepting your offer. This can become a very stressful transaction for you. Once again, go in prepared. There are times that it is impossible to be completely prepared, but you should know if you are ready or not. A recent study by the Center for Responsible Lending predicted that as many as 1 in 5 subprime borrowers who took out reduced-payment, low-documentation mortgages between 1998 and mid-2006 could lose their homes because of steep payment increases and penalties they can't handle (Kenneth Harney, Washington Post 2007). Do you believe that with these numbers, a serious opportunity can and will present itself? You bet it will!

Help your own cause by using technology. Send your initial request via e-mail to the lender if at all possible. It will cut out the "phone tag" game. If the lender is non-responsive within a couple of business days of your initial request, move on. You do not have time to waste waiting for others to respond. Conversely, if you fail to respond to a lender's request, do not attempt to play "hot potato" by dropping the information they had been requesting in their lap at the last minute, without respecting their time. We're probably negotiating with a bank, escrow company, or attorney, while we are responding to e-mail as well. Both authors of this book get along so well as we have a joint philosophy of getting any request done as quickly as possible, even if it means cutting into personal time. We're both compulsive about this. You should be, too, to become a successful investor in foreclosures.

The Deal Went Through—Now What?

Assuming that the deal goes through or that you are certain that you want to buy a property and have an accepted offer, you need to finalize your cash flow estimates for rental properties based on market rent analysis. This is called rental comps, and you can find them online. One tool that we like to use is www.rentometer.com, mentioned in the previous section, which tells people if they are underpaying or overpaying for a place. It gives you great maps and asks for inputs such as the city, state, address, number of units in the property, the number of bedrooms in the units, and then relies on user data for comps. For you, the investor or homeowner, it also tells you what others are paying, and may help you price right.

Another option is to find a property manager before you buy the home and find out what he/she expects. We recommend dropping the rent slightly if it means you'll rent the place out substantially faster.

The seller should provide a copy of the rent rolls for the property so you know what they have been charging. Ask for this early on. If they are selling the property because of other investments, that is perfectly understandable, but you'll want to understand their motivation. Be cautious of sellers who are unwilling or unable to provide this in a timely manner. A recent seller provided two weeks to close on a transaction that needed to close for "tax reasons" but failed to provide any rent verification. Sure enough, the rents were significantly below market value, and below the seller's initial disclosure. The deal still moved forward as the property was undervalued, but it was not as great of a deal as initially proposed. This is a long-term buyer; if you are as well, this type of deal makes a great deal of sense.

> Dani has made many great investment decisions, but she made a mistake in Texas. She wanted to hit her number and knew from the rental comps it was possible. It was, but she had to hold out two months to make $75 per month extra. This means it cost her $2000 in lost rent, and she had a return on investment on that deal of 26.66 months! She should have dropped it $75 and just taken a hit on the rent. A good example of "Don't be penny wise and pound foolish," to use an old cliché.

Appraisers are another great resource, as they will typically conduct a rental survey as part of their appraisal process. Some more experienced ones will do the rental survey for a fee before doing the appraisal itself.

Another caveat: Be sure you get it in writing that the tenant will allow you or your agent to show the property. You do not want to waste valuable time you could be selling it because the tenant is stubborn. Property managers advise tenants of their rights even if you are their client; that is, even though the property managers are paid by *you*, they will often tell tenants they do not have to show the property because some potential tenants will not rent if they do, and the property manager will not collect their percentage of the rent that month. Avoid this if at all possible and get it in writing and inform the tenants up front, even if it means a month-to-month lease.

Another scam? The property manager owning the maintenance company that happens to charge more than other maintenance companies. Some people might call this laundering. In fact, Dani found evidence of a property manager charging both her *and* the tenant for the *same* service! Be careful of these kinds of things.

Gotcha's in the Foreclosure Market

As you've seen in the previous five chapters, the foreclosure market is more complicated than the traditional home buying process. As a result, there are a lot of potential "gotcha's" you need to look out for, and it is our job to warn you of them—at least as many as we can. We will start with common mistakes that investors make, and what to do to avoid them. Then we will move into the actual property itself, and things to watch out for.

Common Mistakes the Foreclosure Investor Makes and How to Avoid Them

You are no doubt in a hurry to close the deal, and we do not blame you—in fact, we encourage it. But, you must do your research and you must do it well. This is particularly true of the title policy. You will need to be sure the title is clear, and this means right up to the day you take ownership. You do not want last-minute liens filed that you will have to pay. Work with a reputable title company even though they tend to be quite expensive. Your lender can recommend several sources with years of experience in the business. Part of this process is to get a title insurance policy.

Not Acting Quickly

Another big mistake is not act quickly enough. Once you find the property in the area with the specs you are looking for, you need to move on it. If you think you are the only one looking, ask foreclosure sites that see millions of hits per month! These people aren't visiting the sites for fun; they want a good deal just like you do. They also want a hotter market, just like you do. Once you find the deal you want, follow our steps and carry through with your deal. The early bird definitely gets the worm in the foreclosure market. There are always plenty of worms, but maybe not the one you like. Jump on it when you see it, especially if you are going to live in the house. Many people do not look at their primary home the same way they do investment property and there are often different criteria for your purchase beyond just pure financial gain (although that is nice, too).

Annoying the Owners

Do not annoy or insult the owner—they still own the property! We've seen it before, and it gets you nowhere. The owners of homes in foreclosure can be extremely frustrating to work with, but put yourself in their shoes. They may feel embarrassed, ashamed, or inadequate, especially if they have a family. They may feel like they have failed, and here you are, Ms. Money Bags, coming in to take their home from them for lower money than it is worth—a home they may have owned for awhile and they are attached to, saw their children grow up in, whatever the situation. It is often emotional, tumultuous, frustrating, and sad for the owners. If you insult them, annoy them with phone calls, make them feel lower than they already are feeling, or treat them in a lesser way than you'd want to be treated in this situation, you are sure to lose the deal, not to mention kick someone while they are down.

While this is a business deal for you and we aren't the "touchy feely" types, we do believe that it is not only in your best interest to avoid annoying and/or insulting the owner, but it is also the right thing to do. Bill's family's first home was a foreclosure where he knew the previous owner's kids; they were the neighborhood bullies! Bill's family certainly did not want to be known as the people buying the home that the bullies' family lived in for 20 years until both parents lost their jobs in the aerospace industry. They moved forward with the transaction with a certain level of fear of the previous owners.

Not Following Up

Failing to follow up is another big mistake we see investors make. As noted earlier in this book, sometimes it takes several mailings, mailings followed up with calls, on-site visits, or a real estate agent pushing, for a deal happen. Sometimes, when the first postcard or first letter arrives or you make the first phone call, the owner is still in disbelief. Following up and keeping track as the home proceeds through the process will save you a lot of time and headache. Also, if the home becomes current and is no longer an at-risk home, you do not want to waste your time pursuing it— so following up with your research is just as important as following up with the owners.

Let's not forget about the banks. They may turn down your first offer, but as auction time nears or REO time becomes closer, that may change. Bill has seen banks turn down a transaction over a $2,000 difference; of course, they do not tell the buyer or investor the amount is so minimal, just that the "offer does not work." Without disclosing the specific terms on this transaction, I can tell you that the difference that made the deal work to everyone's benefit was a couple hundred dollars. The understanding of the process, combined with the established relationship, made the difference for all of the parties involved.

Not Performing Due Diligence

Failing to perform due diligence is another huge risk for investors. This means securing lending, researching the area, following proper procedures, talking to the right people at the bank, and hiring the right people for your side of the transaction (attorneys if needed, appraisers, inspectors, title companies, etc). Do your homework! Spend some money on appraisals, inspections, and any other critical items so you know that the deal makes sense. It is better to back out of a deal and lose a small earnest deposit, or some other insignificant amount than follow through with a deal that will cost you a lot more in the long run. While this is important for all transactions, it becomes absolutely critical when you are buying properties that you have never seen, in states that you may never even fly over, let alone set foot in. Again, certain areas will not take kindly to your investing in their area, as you will be viewed as the outsider that is increasing their market values for them. Interesting that people want the equity, but don't want the prices raised in their own communities, isn't it? Do your homework, and the locals will end up on your side, while creating some wealth for yourself.

Avoiding a Home Inspection

Failure to invest in a home inspection is another "gotcha" that investors often make, especially if they are the do-it-yourself (DIY) type. A few hundred dollars for an inspection could save you thousands! Homes can have a ton of problems that inspectors can find that you perhaps cannot.

Establish a budget based on your financial knowledge, as well as your ability to make repairs (or hire contractors to do repairs). Add a buffer of at LEAST 10 percent if you have experience, or even more if you are just starting. It is better to have more money left over for saving or reinvestment, rather than having to keep funding a project just because you must finish it.

Do not rely on just your own visual inspection, unless you yourself are an inspector or contractor. Realize that you are buying an asset at a significant discount already, so spend a little money to make sure it is the right asset. Be sure to note and jot down everything you see or worry about as a potential risk factor or problem and follow up until every issue is dealt with or identified satisfactorily; expect to perhaps even take some time off of work to do all of this right. Depending on the level of discount you are receiving on the home, or if you are purchasing directly from the buyer who just defaulted on their payments, you still want to know what needs to be repaired. This is a double-edged sword.

To the banks, the home is a liability once they own it; as long as it gets off their books, they do not care what needs to be repaired and may help by offering incentives to buy it. To the current owner, as mentioned earlier, do not offend them by "nit-picking" every little item that they failed to maintain or repair. A recent investor was asked to "balance" the ceiling fan in a unit that he was selling significantly under market along with closing cost assistance to the buyer. While he is extremely laid back, and very easy-going, this sent him to the edge and almost caused him to cancel the transaction. Do not become this type of investor or buyer. You will greatly limit your ability to succeed.

Undercapitalization

Failure to capitalize correctly is another major issue to consider. While this becomes less of an issue for more experienced investors, this can be a huge issue for those just getting started. While it is understood that you are purchasing built-in equity, the cash flow necessary to make up the deal can add up quickly. As mentioned throughout the book, the cost of improvements and repairs can add up quickly. If you do not believe the written word on this one, tune in to "Flip This House" on the A&E television network. You will see the many unexpected surprises that come up, even with an experienced investor. You will consistently hear from this group on television "fall in the love with the numbers first, then the house" (www.aetv.com; 2007). Remember, this is not a get-rich-quick scheme, but it is also not a "let's figure out as we go along" scenario, unless you intend on making a lot less money than you are capable of making. Knowledge and understanding is the key.

Inexperienced Agents

While we aren't opposed to working with a real estate agent through the deal, we are definitely opposed to working with inexperienced agents, sales counselors, or other individuals who at the bare minimum have not received their higher licensing credentials. Recently, a client of Bill's had received his first notice of default from the bank, which he had already cured a couple of days prior. On a given Saturday morning, he received three phone calls from real estate "professionals" who had buyers looking for a home in his area, as well as an "angel investor" who could help their situation. Never mind that the client was at least $40K in negative equity, they could do it.

This couple was provided with three questions to ask the investors and real estate agents to gauge their level of experience, and found that each and every one of them skirted around the real issue and their ability to help. Case in point—there are plenty of experienced real estate agents that know how to work foreclosure deals, know how to avoid the issues we're talking about here, and know the process that can walk you through every step and protect you with a good contract. Inexperienced "professionals" aren't going to have the skill to look out for you, as well intentioned as they may truly be, and even a darn good residential agent that isn't a foreclosure specialist is one to be wary of, in our opinion. Recently, a top agent in Southern California acknowledged that he could not imagine how quickly the market turned, and how he had to re-educate himself to the changing marketplace, as he had not dealt with foreclosures and short sales in over ten years. His experience and knowledge is deep enough that he will quickly adapt. The truth is, those with experience can change and adapt, while those that lack knowledge and experience can guide their clients down a very difficult path that they may not be able to appropriately help them out of. (This is well explained, by the way, in the book *Commissions at Risk* by Danielle Babb.)

Certainly, those real estate agents that are comfortable with their performance and knowledge will understand the point that we are illustrating

Finding the facts

Interview the real estate agents and financiers that you will be working with as if they were attorneys or medical professionals. You want to deal with specialists, not general practitioners.

here, while others will complain and moan that their job is made more difficult by having clients interview them, when they could be working on the next deal. Ironically, if all of their clients came by referral, their next deal would be waiting to speak with them. If their knowledge were that of a specialist instead of a generalist, they'd be hiring additional staff to keep up with the business!

Lender Problems

Lending problems are another big issue and often *the* stumbling block for closing the deal. Dani has worked with the best of lenders, but still has run into issues that have created problems like a four-month closing period and *very* upset sellers. In fact, one deal that would have turned out quite nicely was lost due to lending problems. Many banks are outsourcing functions, taking a long time to close, finding "last-minute" issues that need to be resolved, or the representative isn't giving you the full information up front. Case in point: Dani had a loan due to close at the end of October that ended up being delayed—even though it *had* to close by then because the construction loan was due and payable on the 31st. She got a notice of "entire balance due" and the lender still dragged its feet on the permanent loan. The final loan closed on the absolute last day the loan could have gone into default, in spite of the fact Dani had done everything correctly. She had gotten everything the bank needed to them literally on day one of the loan application! She was given an "approval," (which by the way means absolutely nothing), only to have them ask for ridiculous things like a letter from her accountant that she really did own a business and taught for schools, and that a small credit card bill really was paid off despite the fact she'd already proven that two months prior. The situation endangered her credit status and was incredibly stressful.

Sometimes these situations are out of our hands, so you need to stay on top of your lenders and your representative. Make sure they are giving you the real information; not what you want to hear so you won't annoy them for the next week. Get everything in writing, including your Good Faith Estimate, which will include everything payable and should be written in good faith—meaning it is as accurate as the lender can possibly be and it is based on your credit score and your contingencies. Lender issues can wreak so much havoc that sellers back out, and if they have other (perhaps better) offers, they may use it as an excuse to go with someone else. Use a representative that you know will come through.

Finding the facts

It is imperative to provide a complete and thorough financial package up front to avoid unnecessary delays in closing. It is better to prepare for the worst, and expect the best, when dealing with foreclosure investment, as Murphy's Law is very much in play when dealing with real estate. Consider having your documents always scanned and ready at a moment's notice.

As with real estate agents, your lender should be interviewed, though in this area you will know much sooner as most are looking for the deal that makes them the most money, rather than the deal that makes the most sense for you. You will know if the financing is too exotic for your tastes. Now, this is not to say that you shouldn't listen to your lenders' recommendations. Some of the most difficult deals Bill has dealt with are because the borrower did not listen to his recommendation, and ended up being penalized for closing later than scheduled. For example, you are an experienced investor, yet you believe that you should only use fixed-rate loans in purchasing your properties. With this belief, you are severely affecting your ability to buy properties and build your portfolio. You are also pricing yourself out of certain types of homes. Think of purchasing multi-unit properties on a fixed rate—you will certainly need to place 30 percent down or greater to have what you consider to be a comfortable monthly payment. (Remember cash flow!) In addition, you are purchasing a home, failing to disclose all of your liquid assets, when lo and behold, it appears that you are short on money to close the deal. Now you need to prove that you really have more money than you mentioned—try to explain that one!

As the market continues to change, lenders will continue to tighten their lending standards. As Dani's experience indicates, lenders will come up with what are often ridiculous requests at the very end, because the automated systems that condition for specific items (which are correctly provided well in advance) are questioned by an underwriter or a closing manager who does not want to be the one on the hook if and when the mortgage defaults. Everyone is trying to cover their behind, causing the customer undue stress and delay. Avoid this situation by providing all of your items as quickly as possible, and more importantly than anything, make sure that they are reviewed within a couple of days of being provided. Failure to do this is often one of the primary causes for last-minute fire drills. Ten days before the actual closing date, ensure that your lender is prepared to close on the scheduled date. Although it puts some additional pressure on the lenders, it buys them the additional time necessary in case of delays on any other parties involved, and protects you as the consumer against surprises, and worse, the expiration of your rate commitment from the bank (particularly if rates increased). The point is there are several legitimate and several careless reasons why your deal may not close on time. You may not be able to control the legitimate reasons, but you can avoid careless ones. As mentioned before, do not play "hot potato" with your mortgage and the required conditions, and you will not get burned in the end.

> Research overlay, redevelopment, and office placement zones to see where the money will be spent in the coming years. You can bet that if Home Depot, Lowes, or a Marriott hotel (of any brand) is set for construction in the next 12-18 months, that they have done extensive research on the demographics for that area. Always follow the money.

Finding the facts

Area Specific Issues

There are also area-specific issues to consider. Among ones the authors have faced (and there are certainly more, which we will discuss):

- *Major companies moving out of the area.* This means jobs (and residents) may go with them. Research the local business journals, or on chamber of commerce web sites to get a head's up on this. You should be acutely aware that job growth is highly promoted, while downsizing or relocations are not, so you'll need to read between the lines and do some further investigating.

- *Major companies or universities moving into an area*. This will create demand—a great thing! Purchase three months to a year before the movement starts; it is the best time to buy.

- *The view from the backyard*. If it is a view of other homes, fine. If it is a view of something less than desirable, reconsider.

- *Flood plains or flood zones*. Having to pay ridiculous flood insurance rates can severely eat into profits. Dani had two properties next to one another. One was not in a flood plain, so when she bought the home next door, she assumed it wasn't either. To close escrow, she had to pay $4,000 in flood insurance. Talk about a surprise! As she tried to get out of the deal, she learned that some flood insurance is transferable. The previous owner had $450 per year flood insurance and she was able to transfer it to her name and continue to pay that premium. Understand—this took more than five hours of phone calls, a lot of runaround, and a lot of research. Be prepared in case of issues like this. The more you read of others experiences and the more experience you get on your own, the more you'll know what to look out for and the more 'second nature' this will become. The model for determining flood insurance is so outdated (and only costs $11 per search) that you can't expect it to be very accurate. Challenge the findings; you'll be surprised how easy it is to win.

- *Dropping income levels*. This is an indicator that the area's image and appeal could plummet. Research online; this information can be found on most city or county websites. Look for a three-year trend in incomes.

- *How well the neighbors keep their homes up and what percentage of them are renters*. You can find all this demographic data online.

Author's Notes

Dani purchased three spec homes in Tucson, Arizona without first seeing them. When she went to visit, she found that all three homes had great views— of the nearby cemetery. Great for the Halloween-loving crowd, but it made it more difficult to sell the properties.

The higher percentage of renters, the more of an investor area it will be; meaning that more investors than homeowners may want to buy there. While investors drive prices up quickly, they also can suck the life out of a market as easily by pulling their money out quickly.

- *Cheap housing.* This may lead to a bad rental market—if someone can buy a house for the same price as the rent, why would they rent? Some people cannot buy due to poor credit. Look for areas with "Section 8" housing; they are not necessarily poor investments if the area is not in a predominantly crime-ridden area, and the government will guarantee your rental income. Dani has good cash flow on properties in Arizona in Section 8.

- *Rental restrictions.* If you are buying property in an area of the country where there is a large population of illegal aliens, beware of changing county laws (particularly in Texas) that disallow you to rent to them. Undocumented immigrants are a heavy percentage of our rental population in border states and if you are buying in these areas, this may affect your cash flow more than you think. Imagine purchasing an investment property, then being told how much you can charge (rent control) and to whom you may or may not rent.

- *Association fees.* Be sure you know what they are, and what the penalties are if something goes astray.

- *Noise.* People who are renting generally do not mind construction in their area, but people who are buying do not want to hear the noise all day. This is also the case for properties near an airport or airbase. The sound of Air Force jets and commercial airliners reduce property value.

> Dani owns properties that belong to associations and she is not opposed to them, as they do serve a purpose. However, she notes that first, as a property owner, you will usually have to cover association fees, not the tenant, and second, sometimes associations are just ridiculous. One association fined her $100 every time a shrub died. They also wouldn't let her real estate agent put up signs, so they had to be put in the window of the home where the association couldn't do anything—though they still tried!)

- *High crime zones.* These areas are tough to resell in. Look for lower crime rates; you can get this information relative to the national average online. Check out the Yahoo Demographics site, which has some great information about zip codes as they relate to the national average. Redevelopment areas are the exception, as the government is committing to improving them.
- *Toxic waste or landfill issues.* Yes, believe it or not homes have been built in toxic waste sites or on top of landfills, which may drastically affect the value of your home. Find out first!
- *Overlay zones for multi-use zoning.* This is another buzzword to look for. This is the pre-cursor to a redevelopment area, without inciting local politics. These are great purchase and expansion opportunities for investors.
- *Curb appeal.* Check out how the property looks now or, since you are buying foreclosures, its potential for curb appeal with some work. Paint and landscaping are easy fixes but make a home look absolutely run down if not properly maintained. Look for these eyesores purposely! If you are dealing with a homeowner's association, be prepared to choose from their color palette.
- *Taxes.* Property taxes in some areas are steeper than others and some are really steep. In California, watch out for Mello Roos, an added tax imposed on property owners in districts that are financing public facilities or improvements, which can add upwards of one full percentage point. When buying foreclosures, make sure there are no tax liens against the property too, and if a private builder built the home, make sure there are no builder liens. Additionally, large builders may include in the fine print a Private Transfer Tax of .5 to 1 percent of the sales price

Author's Notes

When Dani first bought property in Texas and decided to impound the taxes and insurance, she saw the bill for 2.7 percent. She thought her California property taxes were high at 1.7 percent! It really caused a lot more headache and she does not make as much on those homes due to the incredibly high tax. Other areas are even higher.

that will affect you in areas that do not appreciate as quickly as the coastal or high density communities.

- *Occupation or investment.* As a foreclosure investor, you'll want to decide if you're going to live in the home for two years so you can take the $250,000 tax exemption on capital gains ($500,000 if married), or if you want to rent it out right away. Talk with a tax accountant or tax attorney about the rules and regulations on this, and find out about converting rental property to a primary residence. Also, what you intend to do with the property will impact what you're willing to pump into it in repairs.

> Always consider the area you are investing in; it may have a large impact on the appraisal value as well as the level of appreciation, or even depreciation, that can be expected in the coming months or years of ownership.

Finding the facts

- *Mixed-use areas.* Areas with heavy concentrations of residential mixed with multi-use or commercial, or experiencing heavy transition are great purchases. For example, a tear-down residence in California is appraising for $350,000 in an area where commercial lots are appraising for over $1 million. Do you think we will buy it as an investment?

- *Land investments.* Look for a manufactured home sitting on a minimum of five acres. A savvy real estate agent will attempt to price it to account for the home; buy it for the land, especially if it is in a rapidly growing area.

Issues With the Property Itself

While we've been pretty fortunate with not finding damage we weren't aware of prior to buying homes, it happens and many of our friends have run into these unfortunate circumstances. Be sure that your home inspector knows what he/she is doing. Preferably, your inspector will have extensive experience in construction, particularly residential, and they will know exactly what to look for. Look for major potential problems, plumbing or electrical issues, foundation and roofing issues, and mold.

With mold, people assume the worst and automatically want it fixed or will not buy at all. Make sure it gets cleaned up before you buy and if possible at the banks or the owners' expense.

In particular, banks want these issues resolved before closing. Be prepared to fork over the dough for all of the repairs that you need, which means calculating this into the cost. Make sure the kitchen appliances work, and that the home is structurally sound. If the home has not been occupied for over 30 days, ensure the plumbing is checked; water tends to stagnate and corrode old pipes and they can burst. If the home does not have all copper piping, you may have to note this on a sale agreement, so look for that. Also, check for things that seem minor but may be costly, like broken windows, dishwashers, or water heaters.

You want a thorough home inspection, with specific descriptions and pictures to support the areas of concern. You should make a list from the inspector of everything you want repaired, along with its estimated cost. Chances are the bank will not do it, but they may be willing to deduct the repairs from the price. Even if they do not, you may still want the property, but you need to go in with your eyes wide open and this is the best way to do that.

Author's Notes

Dani bought a home that was three years old. Two tenants in three years kept the home up beautifully, but the property manager slacked on the third tenant. When Dani went to sell the property, her real estate agent—after finally getting in to see the property—said that the house smelled like animal and human urine and feces. The property was also damaged from the tenants leaving trash piled up over a foot high and filling the back yard like a landfill. Not exactly a way to sell the house. She had to kick the renters out, clean up the house, and take a hit on the mortgage each month before she could put it on the market. In the meantime, the cash flow was negative.

Beware of Existing Tenants

Beware of bad tenants. If the home has been occupied by renters and the homeowners have not lived in the area or the property manager has not done a good job, there is a chance that the home will be in need of serious cleaning—carpet replacement, painting, etc. Also, beware that once you rent the house out, the tenants may want things done like fences built, landscaping taken care of, etc. Decide ahead of time if it is in your budget, and then let tenants know before they sign the lease. Use a great property manager—it makes all the difference in the world. It is hard to screen tenants for their cleanliness, but try to establish a gut instinct (which we've found to be most accurate) as well as the usual credit checks, employment checks, etc.

THE ROLE OF THE INTERNET

THE INTERNET HAS PUT PRESSURE ON EVERY SINGLE MARKET, COMPANY, AND business in the world. It has globalized and revolutionized our world, has created a nation of instant gratifiers, and has put the squeeze on many companies by creating a market almost solely based on price. Web sites have certainly streamlined the real estate business. Aggregator sites, MLS listing sites, loan comparison sites, the ability to get credit scores, comparative analyses, and even list your own home online have changed the real estate market forever. What many didn't predict (although one company most definitely did, and we'll talk about them in Chapter 8) is that technology would also streamline the foreclosure business.

Foreclosures—A Business

First, yes, foreclosures are a business; not only for investors, but for the many people involved in the process. Before the internet, most people didn't know about foreclosures or how to find them. In the 1980s, it wasn't uncommon to phone a bank to ask about foreclosures but it was a very clumsy and time-consuming process. Banks were a bit more desperate to dump properties that they didn't want due to incredibly high interest rates, which isn't necessarily the case today. People would scour newspapers or talk to "friends of friends"

Finding the facts

The internet has changed the way almost every business does business. It has leveled the playing field for small-time investors to compete and find killer deals—just like the big guys.

but most people didn't have access. This has changed dramatically, creating a truly global marketplace in foreclosure investment.

Imagine spending a couple of hours each day searching for opportunities, simply by having the tools available to you online. Those who know Bill well understand that coffee houses are his favorite place to relax—

and do some investment research. Banks also use technology to manage the default process, and even to make arrangements for homeowners. Investors and lenders can list and even exchange foreclosed properties online. "Default service" divisions and asset management departments at banks also help to streamline the process and make it more efficient—and this information is readily accessible to anyone with internet access.

Unfortunately, the ability for banks to quickly list homes has also created a market where people are not seeing as great of deals as they did in the 80s and 90s; however, with bank-owned inventory rising due to owners being unable to make inflated payments, this is predicted to change soon. Since foreclosed homes take longer to sell, they will continue to exert downward pressure on the price of the home; at the same time, the banks liability continues to increase as the interest continues to accumulate. New web sites even let lenders identify borrowers who may be in need of assistance, to help them find an agent to quickly sell their home at a price less than what is owed; the best possible scenario if in fact the owner is facing foreclosure. As we noted earlier, this is known as a short sale.

Web v2—Changing the Hunt for Foreclosures

Many of you have heard of Web version 2.0, and we already discussed a bit about what it is and what it isn't—and more importantly, how it is changing things in the marketplace. It is also significantly changing the real estate industry, one of the last service sectors to be affected by the web. While the role of the real estate agent will change drastically (discussed thoroughly in Dani's book *Commissions at Risk*), it also is affecting the foreclosure markets. Web 2.0 has let the cat out of the bag with an incredible influx of new information and great data available to the average consumer or investor, all with a user interface that is not only easy to understand and follow but also is dynamic and changes with your needs and preferences. In this chapter we're going to talk about the internet's new role in foreclosure deals, including in searching for, lending on, and valuing homes. We'll talk about can't-miss sites, and partnering with online companies. We'll also talk about the benefits of closing the deal online and the role that will play in the future.

The Internet's New Role in Foreclosure Deals

The internet has led to incredible new ways to find foreclosure properties online and in all stages of the process. Many sites offer the ability to search and find foreclosures, but we only really recommend one, which we talk about extensively in the next chapter. We'll discuss some of the others, and our opinions on what benefit they provide and what they lack for a moment. These sites are for the searching component and how-to component of finding foreclosures.

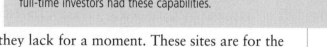

Several years ago, no one realized the impact the internet would have on the foreclosure markets. Systems allowing individuals to search for foreclosures at every stage have revolutionized the foreclosure markets, and made it a business in itself. Before the web, only institutional or full-time investors had these capabilities.

- **Foreclosures.com** An interesting approach, but not a lot of public information. The site owner takes a unique approach in that she appears to believe we have an obligation to behave a certain way in our approach to buying foreclosures. While we have nothing against her viewpoint and certainly we believe that owners should be treated with respect, we believe her approach is a bit too extreme and perhaps blends two ideologies that are seemingly impossible to combine. There isn't much free information, and even attending 'webinars' costs money, which many other sites provide for free. Most of the site appears to be dedicated to selling product. For seven days, you can get information on various properties; the payment covers e-mail alerts, finding auctions and REO lists, gaining access to the foreclosure websites, and a subscription to a newsletter. Beyond that, not much is offered that is of use.

- **RealtyTrac.com** This is the site we recommend overall, and we'll talk more about it in Chapter 8. It is by far the most comprehensive, fully integrated site we have used.
- **Biggerpockets.com** This site is more of an information resource, and it is one we recommend checking out. It will tell you how to find foreclosures through the Recorder's offices and through other online sites but from what we can find, it isn't a full solution site.
- **Searchsystems.net** This is strictly a public records database. Yes, it does include property records, but you have to do a lot of digging and pay to get anything useful. You can register through a full service site and get far more information.
- **Foreclosure.com** This site is interesting. For one thing, it shows you live auctions. The site actually has quite a bit of information online and it does give you the status as well as some information. We've found it most useful to take the information and plug it into Zillow or another major home valuation site to see what the property may be worth. For example, we found a home up for auction with three days left at $19,000 that Zillow estimated to be worth $60,000. If you got it for $19,000 and there wasn't much work to be done, it wouldn't be a bad deal. This site estimates price using the Zestimate, which is Zillow's tool. This site gives you a seven-day trial, and we do like the live auction feature that gives you the e-mail address for the broker or real estate agent.
- **Hudhomesnow.com** This is another seven-day trial site. This site give you access to foreclosed homes, and something many others do

not—HUD homes and VA homes (those backed by the government that are being foreclosed upon). It also gives you access to auctions, bankruptcies, repossessions, and other distressed properties, such as for tax lien purposes. This is a site worth looking into.

- **Bankhomesdirect.com** This is a RealtyTrac site. It provides great access to homes that are easy to search for. This site helped one of the authors find out that a home on the street adjacent to where the author lives really wasn't being sold in the traditional sense as believed, but was actually a foreclosure. This site is free, and includes detailed property information on over 400,000 bank-owned homes across the country. This is one of the more comprehensive sites though giving you lien information and other public record data on one screen.

> There is really no reason to sign up for multiple systems. Choose the one of most value to you and become intimately familiar with its setup and opportunities.
>
> *Finding the facts*

- **Buybankhomes.com** When we called Washington Mutual to inquire about a property listed on this web site as owned by the bank (REO status), they said the property was not in fact owned by the bank. The representative recommended this site as a way to find homes that were accurately represented. While we didn't find the site particularly helpful, apparently the banks feel it is accurate.
- **Defaultresearch.com** This site has updated information on default properties that shows up within days, not weeks; information appears to be updated very quickly. Similar to RealtyTrac information, but with very limited geographic coverage.
- **All-Foreclosure.com** Though not well publicized, this is a very detailed site that is easy to use. It was a pleasant surprise to find it!

The Internet and Lending

The internet also plays a role in the lending process. Not only can you find hard money lenders online (do a Google search for "hard lending AND foreclosures") but also you can, in many cases, have a standard 30-day escrow in which you can find a bank that will do a high loan-to-value loan on the property. Companies like Lending Tree and E-LOAN have changed the way you can find and secure lending online. Two other sites, quicken-loans.com and capitalonehomeloans.com, play a role in comparing mortgages and applying online. In addition, many banks offer online applications including Wells Fargo, Countrywide, Washington Mutual, and Bank of America, among many others. However, none of them can provide specific recommendations regarding your individual criteria.

Upon an initial search, some providers will entice you with an extremely low rate that has a cost of five points, while others show you a more realistic rate that requires a significant down payment of 30 percent or greater. Regardless of which provider you decide to use, ensure that you are using verifiable information so that the rate and terms you were looking for will be close to the terms you will actually receive. Knowing that the markets change on a daily basis, you will begin to see the trends with what is occurring as you search on a regular basis. You can also look at Bankrate.com, as this is another well-known resource to use when searching for lending options. You should, however, be cautious—many of the companies that advertise on the specific sites tend to be call centers that focus on handling general transactions.

We highly recommend that you work with people or companies that you know, as you must have direct contact or access to the individual or company that is assisting in your financing of the property. You may be weeks into a transaction when you realize that you are speaking to a team of processors, all of whom have their own opinion of your qualifications. All of the research that you have done is wasted if they cannot write the deal for you; do you think they'll cover your equity loss or the forfeiture of your deposit because you could not get approved? Hardly.

The internet is a great resource for research at this time but, as far as lending is concerned, has not yet become all encompassing in its ability to deliver customized solutions. Expect this to change in the coming years.

As far as available information, there is plenty out there. A recent Google search shows that if you are looking for foreclosures, there are over 26 million items that come up; that is prohibitive amount of information to even scan through. Through experience, research, and our own personal use of technology, we have sifted through most of this information for you in this book. As the amount of information posted online can expand greatly in a very short amount of time, we are confident that new players may come up on a regular basis, though we are using proven individuals and organizations. Any and all of the data and contacts in this publication have been used by the authors on a regular basis.

Valuation and the Web

Another great place to start your research is in the valuation phase, as valuing a home is a critical component in the process. Not only will you need to know the appraiser's value, but you'll also want to know what other homes in the area are selling for. There are several tools you can use to do that. RealtyTrac includes an estimated value range and estimated property value on most of the properties in its database. Zillow is one of our overall favorites for getting started, and here are some others, as the information always needs to be double checked:

- www.zillow.com

- www.cmafacts.com

- www.easyhomevaluation.com

- www.housevalues.com

- www.cravonline.com (Center for Responsible Appraisal & Valuation)

- www.homegain.com

Note that these aren't always accurate and they reflect previous closings, not what the home is actually worth today or what someone is willing to pay for it. That number could be lower or higher and is dependent on many factors. We have added the Center for Responsible Appraisal and Valuation site as a reference point to look at the concerns outlined from a national perspective. While we believe that much of their information is not specific enough to help, the content that is outlined solidifies our rationale for insisting that you do your homework. Remember that you are looking for specific data regarding the home you want to purchase as that valuation is the most important to you, while the comparative market analysis that is done by a real estate agent is designed to help you understand how your home is placed in its respective marketplace. In other words, an appraisal

Be careful of web-based appraisals that are based on online listings or on estimates not provided by appraisers. While the property may be worth that much, appraisers will take into consideration more local information. Online comps are a good place to start, but the bank will require a full appraisal to protect themselves. You should do the same.

or valuation is specific to your investment, while a CMA is generic to the overall area. Knowing you are buying a $150,000 asset in a $125,000 market would be an indicator to walk away (unless you had specific knowledge of some impending event that would change this); conversely, if you were purchasing a $150,000 asset in a $300,000 market, you would be making a more than worthy investment.

Partnering Online

Partnering with one good online foreclosure company is really what we recommend. You need the tool that you choose to be complete and to fit your needs, and you want the information to be accurate. Sometimes, it will take several phone calls to banks before you find a home that was accurately listed, and this can be frustrating. If you have had good success with one company, it is good to stick with them, but you may want to use the seven-day trials that we have talked about throughout this book to try out other options. Be aware that they usually auto-renew and charge your credit card once the seven days are up, so be sure to watch for that in your statement and cancel if you want to. It is not a bad idea to check with multiple sites though and see if they have different information, and to try out several sites to see what works for you. Do not skip the auction sites; they can have great deals and are super convenient.

Close the Deal Using the Internet?

While most companies aren't fully e-signing and e-closing compatible, many are getting there. One company comes to note: SureDocs by A la Mode Inc, out of Oklahoma City, has this functionality to get disclosures signed this way. Various mortgage industry standards are finally taking hold that will allow for easier electronic signing and a more secure method of storing and, perhaps more importantly, authenticating signatures. Certainly, you can shop around online, but be wary of giving out your social security number. Anytime you do this, you may find an inquiry on your credit, which as we discussed earlier may impact your credit score.

You can also find property managers online once you have bought a property. The author's best property managers weren't found through referrals but internet searches. In fact, the referrals turned out to be awful! The internet lets you get real reviews and e-pinions online, something important in today's world, especially if you do not live near the property. Look for property managers online and then phone or email with your list of questions, including if they directly deposit rent. This can be a huge time saver and will help if you're traveling. You can also secure insurance, find insurance carriers, compare insurance rates, and even find flood policies online.

Almost any commodity related to real estate can be researched online. If you are a do-it-yourself type, you can compare the property, the real estate companies, their agents, and every imaginable item that you could ever need for the improvement, renovation, or rehabbing of the property in the comfort of your own home, or on the road as you see fit.

> *Finding the facts*
>
> Hunt online for the best of the best. You can find property managers, appraisers (make sure they are on the banks approved list first), insurance companies, and even escrow companies online. Phone and comparison shop just like you would for anything else!

Partnering in the Foreclosure Market

In this book, we've talked a lot about what to do, how to avoid problems, what to buy, and how to find property. We have mentioned several organizations that provide various services or aspects of the foreclosure purchase process, and we've talked about funding. There is one organization that we highly recommend you work with to manage the process of finding and purchasing foreclosures: RealtyTrac.com. Remember that as an investor and a mortgage banker, we have no particular reason to recommend any organization other than our own experience. We have done our homework and have chosen to recommend this organization to you; let us explain why.

In the foreclosure market, it is important to have up-to-date, relevant, accurate information so that you can act on it and make money. To do this, you need to partner with an organization that has access to the information you need and does not cost you an arm and a leg to do it. We've already talked about the importance of the internet in a model where information changes rapidly, but you also need to have information that is accurate and the names and numbers of trustees and/or attorneys handling the cases. You need dynamic sites with the ability to store information. We've checked out many, and RealtyTrac is the only one that consistently provides accurate information and has all of the data you need to make an informed decision (including lien information, taxes, payment history, lender information, the owner, you name it!). We can therefore confidently recommend this particular site as the solution for what you need. It is rare that authors endorse a particular organization, but in this case, it is well-warranted.

We prefer RealtyTrac because of their comprehensive capabilities, from storage of extended searches to data about properties in every stage.

An Introduction to RealtyTrac

Let us back up a bit and give you a little history of the company and further explain the reason we so highly recommend it. RealtyTrac is ranked as the third largest real estate site—period. Yes, this includes the major ones you already know about. This ranking, done by MediaMatrix, is a vital component indicating their success, which has largely been due to the incredible service they provide. They are number 53 on *Inc.* magazine's 2006 Inc. 500 list of the nation's fastest growing private companies, and the 52nd fastest growing technology company on Deloitte's North American Fast 500. They are currently the leader in the online market space for foreclosures because they provide every bit of the information and resources you will need whether you are a real estate agent, a home seeker, or an investor. Their tools let you evaluate and buy properties below market value, and that is important for your success and to hit your targets. This company has been around for more than ten years. They were founded in 1996 and they currently publish the largest and most comprehensive national database of pre-foreclosure

Markets can change, for better or worse, very quickly. Use the internet to stay current on a particular location's vitals during your transaction.

144

and foreclosure information. But they've also integrated this with for-sale-by-owner information, resale properties, and even new construction, which not only lets you compare what you're buying to what is already out there, but truly gives you a one-stop shop for looking for investments or homes to live in. This is one unique aspect to their business model. They have over 1.3 million properties in their database at any given time, and this number is rapidly climbing. They have property reports, productivity tools (such as online file 'cabinets'), and lots of professional resources. So much in fact that Microsoft's MSN chose them to provide foreclosure data to MSN Real Estate. Yahoo! Real Estate (which has a marketing partnership with Prudential Real Estate) and *The Wall Street Journal's* Real Estate Journal also are supplied their data from RealtyTrac, so you're really going directly to the source instead of an intermediary.

An Overview of the RealtyTrac Site

Just for kicks, we looked up properties in Orange County, California, in their system to show you what a listing looks like. See page 146 for the initial report, which we have edited to remove the property location and the owner's information—note that there was a photo in the upper right corner that we also took out, as it could be used to identify the site. As you can see, the foreclosure status is easily identified and in the Local Specialist area there is an individual to contact, if you wish to go that route. The History of Notices is also a clickable link so you can see all notices on the property. Features and photos were also removed for privacy reasons, as was the trustee's information.

What happens when you click on the three major links—the comparable sales report, the lien and loan history, and the MLS Listings? On page 147, we show you what the comparable sales report looks like, shortened. There were about 15 comparable sales reports for this one property. Excellent information! With the information on this page, you can further evaluate this property's current market value by comparing it against 15 properties that have been sold recently in the neighborhood. This is

RealtyTrac's Property Listing (Sample)

⌂ **RealtyTrac®**

| My RealtyTrac | Search | Get Financing | Contact An Agent | FREE Credit Score | Help | Logout |

QuickSearch Enter a City & State or Zip: [_____] search   My Saved Searches: [Select Search ▼]

| <<Back to Search Results | eBooks | Moving Services | FAQs | What's Next |

Enhanced Property Details

Foreclosure Status   Real Estate Owned Pending ▶

Local Specialist

I specialize in foreclosure properties and purchasing homes below market value. My team & I can help you.

Contact Link

1 Property Information   Save Listing to My RealtyTrac

Property ID	00000000	**Square Feet**	1456
Address	X Street City Name, ST 00000	Lot Size	N/A
		Parcel Number	000-00-000
County	County Interactive Map	**Doc Number**	
		Lot Number	16
		Year Built	1994
Type	Single family residence (RSFR)	**Bldg. Price Sq. Ft.**	N/A
Beds	3	**Lot Price Sq. Ft.**	N/A
Baths	2		

[photoHere]

◀ Prev   Next ▶

🌐 **Map This Property**

Road Map   Aerial View   Birds-eye

! History of Notices

2 Determine Property Value & Evaluate Investment Opportunity   Neighborhood Information

Estimated Property Value Range	Estimated Property Market Value	Check MLS Listings
$1,105,000 - $1,127,000	$1,112,000	
A) Check Comparable Sales FREE	B) Check Lien & Loan History FREE	C) View this property on the MLS
Go	Go	Go

3 Foreclosure Information

Default Amt	
Status	Bank Owned
Recorded	10/6/2006
Entered On	11/9/2006
Last Payment	N/A
Opening Bid	N/A
Sale Date	Not Available

4 Foreclosing Loan Information

Loan Balance	$750,000
Loan Date	N/A
Loan Doc #	
Trans Date	
Trans Value	N/A
First Loan Amount	$750,000
Judgment Amount	N/A

5 Tax Assessment Information

Land Total	$765,724
Improvements	$168,276
Assessed Total	$934,000

6 Contact Information

Owner(s) Name	[Owner's Name]
Address	000 Street, City ST 00000 Contact Owner
Lender	Saxon Mortgage, Inc. - Search for lender on Google
Address	Street City, St 00000
Phone	(000)000-0000

Get Your Home Value

Thinking of selling your current home? Just enter your **square footage** and **zip code** to get an instant estimate of your home's market value

Square Feet   Zip Code   [GO]

RealtyTrac's Comparable Sales Report (Sample)

Comparable Sales   Lien & Loan History

Property Snapshot [Property Address] Newport Coast, CA 92657

Owner Name [Owner's Name Here]
Contact Owner
Beds/Baths 4/5
Square Footage 0

Default Amt
Last Payment N/A
Opening Bid N/A
Sale Date Not Available

With the information on this page, you can further evaluate this property's current market value by comparing it against 15 properties that have been sold recently in the neighborhood. Printer-friendly page

Estimated Market Value of this property: N/A

Comparable Sales Data   **View Comparable Sales Map**

① [Property Address] Newport Coast, CA 92657   **Price: $5,200,00**

Proximity (miles)	0	Year Built	
Date	10/28/2005	Lot Area (Sq. Ft.)	0 Square Feet
Price	$5,200,000	Price Code	Full-Computed from Tax
Rooms/Beds/Baths	N/A	Pool	No
Sq. Ft.	0	APN	000-000-000
Price/Sq. Ft.	N/A	Property Type	Single Family Residence

② [Property Address] Newport Coast, CA 92657   **Price: $4,050,00**

Proximity (miles)	0	Year Built	
Date	11/9/2005	Lot Area (Sq. Ft.)	0 Square Feet
Price	$4,050,000	Price Code	Full-Computed from Tax
Rooms/Beds/Baths	N/A	Pool	No
Sq. Ft.	0	APN	000-000-000
Price/Sq. Ft.	N/A	Property Type	Single Family Residence

③ [Property Address] Newport Coast, CA 92657   **Price: $3,900,00**

Need Help? View the Comparable Sales Frequently Asked Questions

RealtyTrac's Lien and Loan History Report (Sample)

Comparable Sales	**Lien & Loan History**

Property Snapshot [Property Address] Newport Coast, Ca 92657

Owner Name [Owner's Name Here]
<u>Contact Owner</u>

Beds/Baths 4/5
Square Footage 0

Estimated Market Value of this property: N/A

Default Amt
Last Payment N/A
Opening Bid N/A
Sale Date Not Available

The information on this page will help you calculate the total debt encumbering this property, allowing you to make an informed decision about whether the property is a wise investment.
<u>Print Lien & Loan History</u>

Lien & Loan History

History of Notices <u>Understanding The History of Notic</u>

Date Recorded	Prop ID	Status	Opening Bid/Balance	Default Amt	Lender	Trustee
5/11/2007	<u>0000000</u>	<u>NOD</u>	$1,730,036.00	$0.00	[Lender Name]	[Trustee Name]

Date Recorded	Prop ID	Status	Opening Bid/Balance	Default Amt	Lender	Trustee
9/7/2006	<u>000000</u>	<u>REO</u>	$1,730,036.00	$0.00	[Lender Name]	[Trustee Name]

Date Recorded	Prop ID	Status	Opening Bid/Balance	Default Amt	Lender	Trustee
6/2/2006	<u>000000</u>	<u>REO</u>	$1,730,036.00	$0.00	[Lender Name]	[Trustee Name]

Tax Lien Information

Our search of public records found no tax liens for this property.

Loan History <u>Understanding the Loan Histor</u>

Need Help? View the Lien & Loan History <u>Frequently Asked Questions</u>

one of the reasons we go so far as to recommend this company for your needs. This information is vital to successful decision making. We show the lien and loan history page on page 148. Please note that, again, we did edit for privacy.

To shorten the notices shown, we removed about three Prior Sale sections and two mortgage report sections, and we removed some of the owner's confidential informa-

The info provided in RealtyTrac is vital to ensure you're making good decisions. Explore their site and system, and learn what options you have to search for properties and, most importantly, evaluate them once you find them!

Finding the facts

tion. So the report you get is even more comprehensive than this! Why is this important? You know there are no tax liens. You know precisely what the owner owes and to whom, when they opened the loan, who bought the home from whom and what they paid, the full loan history (you can see the first and second note in the very beginning), and more. All of this is very relevant and very important when you identify a property or a list of properties you are interested in.

The final tab on the property listing page allows you to check MLS listings in your area. These are homes for sale either by owner, by broker or by the bank; it retrieved over 5,000 homes that were in the same city! On page 150 is a sample of what a few looked like. Please note photos and prices appear on the site but, again for privacy, we do not show them here. Note the "distance from search address." This is very important—you can easily see if it is an immediate neighbor (as the "58, 63, 274 feet" are) or if it is someone down the street or in another community.

What their system does is unique, not only from a consumer viewpoint but from a technical one. They aggregate public record data nationally from local, regional, and national sources, and then update their database daily. The company is the only national foreclosure service with its own team of abstractors who collect the property records directly from county courthouses and recorders' offices. They have their own proprietary applications that no other company has to cleanse and "normalize" the data (scrub the data for inconsistencies and make sure it contains the

RealtyTrac's MLS Listings (Sample)

MLS Search	City Newport Coast State CA ▼ OR Zip Code	MLS SEARCH

Selected Property	**Bank Owned – [Street Address] – Newport Coast , CA 92657** 4 Beds/5 Baths N/A SF Value N/A Balance $1,730,036	RETURN TO THIS PROPERTY

Properties are listed according to their proximity to your selected property.

4706 Listings which met your search!

Search center address: [Street Address], Newport Coast, Ca

[photo here]
$0,000,000
[Street Address]
Newport Coast 92657
4 Bedrooms / 4.50 Baths
4972 SF (approx)
More Details...

(1 of 4706 listings)
Distance from search address: 58 feet
Status: Active

[photo here]
$0,000,000
[Street Address]
Newport Coast 92657
4 Bedrooms / 5 Baths
5017 SF (approx)
More Details...

(2 of 4706 listings)
Distance from search address: 63 feet
Status: Active

[photo here]
$0,000,000
[Street Address]
Newport Coast 92657
5 Bedrooms / 5 Baths
5017 SF (approx)
More Details...

(3 of 4706 listings)
Distance from search address: 274 feet
Status: Active

[photo here]
$0,000,000
[Street Address]
4 Bedrooms / 4.50 Baths
3636 SF (approx)
More Details...

(4 of 4706 listings)
Distance from search address: 543 feet
Status: Active

right data and fields to go seamlessly into their database). This means you'll have fewer errors and fewer homes in the systems that have poor information. Their system is extremely easy to use; in fact, both of us learned to use it in under ten minutes. The database that they use has records from nearly 2,500 United States counties, which covers over 94 percent of all U.S. households. The

> The MLS is a ten-decade old proprietary system! Many believe that companies like Zillow and other "open source" products will be a long-term solution, eventually replacing the traditional MLS.

Finding the facts

system has the largest and most comprehensive lists of pre-foreclosure, auction, foreclosure, FSBO, and new construction properties of any site out there. We also like that you can use the "scout neighborhoods" option, and find neighborhoods within a specified range of your target that hit various appreciation or depreciation rates.

Their system has the ability to search an area within a certain number of miles from a zip code, and the ability to search by property criteria such as square footage, the costs, etc. It would be nice to have the ability to sort by "level of notice of default," to help identify those owners that may be more distressed than others more quickly. We can already do an advanced search by cost (minimum and maximum), city, county, state, whether it is a pre-foreclosure, foreclosure, auction, REO, etc., and the beginning and end dates, but these added features would make the system more usable and our e-mailed searches for new properties better. The scope neighborhood area, when entering a range of ten miles from Newport Beach, CA, showed properties in San Francisco—easily 600 or more miles away. This area could use a little refining. It would also be nice to have our home listed in the MLS if we use their "list your own home" feature (free to RealtyTrac members) and sell our home through their system.

Another reason we recommend RealtyTrac as your solution: When we searched for properties ourselves, the database included everything—and we mean everything. You can see this from the data above. This is property details, photos, and the number of bedrooms, bathrooms, square footage, and lot size. It then appends to the listing financial data that you need to make sound decisions, which includes both a list and a map of comparable sales (comps), estimated property values, outstanding tax liens (very important!) and bankruptcy filings, loans on the property, and neighborhood information. With pre-foreclosure and foreclosure properties, it includes the amount in default, the trustee and lender information where available, auction dates, locations, and the opening bid amount. As the user, you have the ability to e-mail many of the trustees and lenders right from the property listing page, which we've both used a lot when a property is already represented by a broker for the bank.

The site also gives you free daily e-mail notifications of properties that fit your criteria; the RealtyTrac Agent Network,™ which is a national network of pre-screened real estate agents that can help you manage a foreclosure purchase (we mentioned earlier that if you use an agent, he or she must know how to deal with foreclosures!); and the Lender Network, which is a list of pre-screened financial organizations to help with property finance, automated property valuation estimates, notification of bankruptcies and tax liens, credit scoring, mortgage calculators, and miscellaneous financial tools. Yet there is more; it has another great feature for those of you who are a bit intimidated by the process. It has an automated postcard system that lets any member notify an owner of your interest in their property, and coaching and training materials to help you understand how to invest in real estate and how to purchase pre-foreclosure and foreclosure properties. While we still recommend you phone or drop by the property (at least leave the note on the doorstep) and/or visit with the owner if the meter at the top of the page shows they are in a later stage of the foreclosure process, it is still a convenient way to introduce yourself to the owner and talk with potential sellers less aggressively.

RealtyTrac will also give you general information about foreclosure trends in particular areas. For instance, look at the chart on page 153 taken from their Press Release area on foreclosure rates for California. Charts like these make it easy to see what areas are hitting above-national-average foreclosure rates and which counties have how many properties in various stages of foreclosure. In case you are wondering

Los Angeles Area Foreclosure Market Statistics by County—Nov 2006							
Geography	NOD	NTS	NFS	LIS	REO	Total	1 in every # households	National Average
United States	31,027	44,448	5,685	16,263	22,911	120,334	961	n/a
California	16,270	2,451	0	0	527	19,248	635	1.51
Los Angeles MSAD (LA County)	3,777	559	0	0	157	4,493	728	1.32

From www.RealtyTrac.com/ContentManagement/PressRelease.aspx?ItemID=1578

what nationwide statistics looked like for year-end 2006, they have provided that information as well; see pages 154-155.

In their system, you can search by a variety of criteria, including property type, zip code, address, city or county, and you can evaluate the investment entirely online. A new feature on RealtyTrac is the deployment of an integrated map-based searching application, built on Microsoft's Virtual Earth™ technology. Now, for the first time, users can see all of the properties—regardless of property type—in the RealtyTrac database, laid out on a road map or satellite imagery. This shows visually how much foreclosure activity is in a given area, and allows the user to select a starting point, and simply drag and drop the map to find new properties. It also incorporates new aerial photos, which gives users up-close views of the property and the neighborhood. RealtyTrac has partnered with big companies like Experian, HomeGain, MSN, Yahoo, and Google.

Conclusion

As we've pointed out, the process of buying foreclosures is often hit and miss, as you have to actively research what you are looking for, along with staying on top of those homes that have been sold, refinanced, or simply brought current. In the past, foreclosure data was retrieved through either expensive specialized data sources, or sifting through default filings in newspapers, legal books or at courthouse trustee sales. Finding and buying them used to be difficult. A number of online tools

Rate Rank	State Name	Q1	Q2	Q3	Q4	2006 Total	% HH	1 for every #HH	YOY % Change
	US	323,101	272,108	318,355	345,554	1,259,118	1.1	92	42
37	Alabama	358	914	1,215	1,861	4,348	0.2	452	1
26	Alaska	273	219	291	284	1,067	0.5	192	−24
12	Arizona	6,232	5,818	7,505	8,331	27,886	1.3	79	4
16	Arkansas	3A,706	2,383	2,696	2,533	11,318	1.0	104	−2
14	California	29,537	27,606	37,317	47,969	142,429	1.2	86	131
1	Colorado	13,267	11,599	14,374	15,507	54,747	3.0	33	85
17	Connecticut	2,503	3,159	2,634	3,436	11,732	0.8	118	6
43	Delaware	80	106	140	114	440	0.1	780	36
—	Dst. of Columbia	27	33	23	30	113	0.0	2,432	−30
7	Florida	29,636	25,853	40,136	29,096	124,721	1.7	59	2
2	Georgia	24,419	15,309	15,841	20,406	75,975	2.5	41	67
42	Hawaii	134	199	158	182	673	0.1	684	−79
27	Idaho	760	528	675	545	2,508	0.5	210	−9
11	Illinois	13,691	18,690	19,358	20,716	72,455	1.5	67	55
6	Indiana	15,261	10,775	10,836	10,678	47,550	1.9	53	56
35	Iowa	978	526	564	1,377	3,445	0.3	358	64
31	Kansas	600	1,220	1,113	1,186	4,119	0.4	274	116
29	Kentucky	1,423	1,475	2,310	1,915	7,123	0.4	246	43
40	Louisiana	341	375	957	1,241	2,914	0.2	646	−24
48	Maine	43	24	74	56	197	0.0	3,309	42
38	Maryland	1,081	1,153	1,285	1,003	4,522	0.2	474	−12
25	Massachusetts	972	2,335	4,270	8,310	15,887	0.6	165	226*
5	Michigan	22,742	15,188	20,777	22,212	80,919	1.9	52	127
34	Minnesota	1,131	1,355	1,591	1,918	5,995	0.3	345	167
46	Mississippi	237	154	246	405	1,042	0.1	1,218	−45

U.S. Foreclosure Market Report—2006

Rate Rank	State Name	Q1	Q2	Q3	Q4	2006 Total	% HH	1 for every #HH	YOY % Change
20	Missouri	5,014	3,372	4,029	5,284	17,699	0.7	138	53
36	Montana	317	198	229	322	1,066	0.3	387	18
28	Nebraska	740	368	951	975	3,034	0.4	237	47
3	Nevada	5,037	3,499	5,561	6,948	21,045	2.4	41	172
49	New Hampshire	26	34	47	40	147	0.0	3,721	−2
13	New Jersey	10,460	6,745	8,938	13,877	40,020	1.2	83	14
22	New Mexico	1,836	1,776	756	896	5,264	0.7	148	−28
21	New York	13,794	12,733	11,643	13,876	52,046	0.7	148	40
24	North Carolina	7,664	4,862	5,420	4,530	22,476	0.6	157	41
47	North Dakota	65	34	35	43	177	0.1	1,637	7
8	Ohio	22,860	16,041	19,748	22,868	81,517	1.7	59	64
15	Oklahoma	4,727	3,669	4,178	3,012	15,586	1.0	96	15
23	Oregon	2,025	3,952	1,764	1,832	9,573	0.7	152	40
19	Pennsylvania	12,255	7,532	8,943	9,603	38,333	0.7	137	34
33	Rhode Island	9	327	551	390	1,277	0.3	344	3,015*
30	South Carolina	2,552	1,830	1,252	1,321	6,955	0.4	252	−9
45	South Dakota	76	71	80	63	290	0.1	1,115	47
10	Tennessee	11,718	7,459	7,502	10,117	36,796	1.5	67	33
4	Texas	40,236	39,690	39,363	37,587	156,876	1.9	51	14
9	Utah	3,559	3,487	3,289	2,707	13,042	1.7	59	13
50	Vermont	21	15	6	3	45	0.0	6,542	−25
41	Virginia	1,038	870	1,311	1,131	4,350	0.2	664	49
18	Washington	5,399	4,589	4,243	4,296	18,527	0.8	129	25
44	West Virginia	229	197	208	237	871	0.1	970	−15
32	Wisconsin	1,951	1,676	1,796	2,149	7,572	0.3	304	48
39	Wyoming	61	86	126	136	409	0.2	547	64

Title row: U.S. Foreclosure Market Report—2006 (continued)

*Actual year-over-year increase may not be as high due to expanded data coverage in this state.

today make it easy, and in our opinion RealtyTrac is at the top of that list. We firmly believe that they continue to cement their online presence with a significant presence in the local and national media as well—their monthly RealtyTrac US Foreclosure Report™ has been featured in *TIME*, *US News & World Report* and *Money Magazine* as well as on ABC, NBC, CBS, CNN, and NPR. Rather than needing to be an "industry insider" to receive the quality of information necessary to make money, the company has helped level the playing field and is a full solution provider,

Finding the facts

No market is impervious to foreclosures. Often creative financing can get even the wealthiest of individuals into trouble, especially in a softening housing market. Be smart about your foreclosure choices, and try to find properties that put you into an equity position from day one.

which is the primary reason we recommend them over others in the industry (coupled, of course, with our own experience using various sites). For real estate professionals and lenders, RealtyTrac also provides a Microsoft.NET-based Asset Management System that allows them to receive, post, and even accept offers electronically, as well as manage, maintain, and market their properties. Try out this solution—you will be glad you did.

Buying foreclosures and finding the right property whether for an investment or an owner occupied residence can be time consuming and can even be frustrating. Knowing all about the process, the components that go into the deal, and how to work with the owners and banks are all critical steps to having successful transactions. Learn as much as you can, check out the sites and resources that we recommend, and have a good time watching your personal wealth soar—or move into a home that you didn't think you could afford in an area you never thought you'd get into. Be informed, be conscientious, be consistent, and you'll invest your way to success!

GLOSSARY

The glossary is directly quoted by LandAmerica Financial Group, 2006. The company can be accessed online at www.landam.com.

Absolute auction: Auction with no minimum bid amount. Highest bidder wins.

Abstract (of title): A history of all transactions shown in the public records affecting a particular tract of land.

Acceleration clause: A provision in a promissory note that specifies conditions under which the lender may advance the time when the entire debt is secured by the mortgage becomes due.

Adjustable Rate Mortgage (ARM): Mortgage loans under which the interest rate is periodically adjusted, in accordance with some market indicator, to more closely coincide with the current rates.

Affidavit: A written statement made under oath before a notary public or other judicial officer.

Agreement: A legally binding contract between two or more persons.

Appraisal: A report from an independent third party detailing the estimated value of real estate.

Balloon note/balloon payment: A promissory note with amortization payments scheduled for a long term, usually 30 years, but maturing in a shorter term, often five to seven years. It requires a substantial final balloon payment for the remaining principal.

Bankruptcy: A federal court proceeding under the United States Bankruptcy laws where an insolvent debtor either has his estate liquidated and debt discharged, or is allowed to reorganize its affairs under the protection of the bankruptcy court.

Beneficiary: A person or entity that is legally entitled by a will, trust, or insurance policy to receive money or property.

Chain of title: The history of successive ownership and transfer in the title to a tract of land.

Clear title: Real property ownership free of liens, defects, and encumbrances or claims.

Closing (also called settlement): The completion of a real estate transfer, where the title passes from seller to buyer or a mortgage lien is given to secure debt.

Closing costs: Expenses involved in closing a real estate transaction over and above the price of the land.

Clouded title: A land title having an irregularity, possible claim, or encumbrance that, if valid, would adversely affect or impair it.

Contract of sale: Agreement by one person to buy and another person to sell a specified parcel of land at a specified price.

Conveyance: The transfer of title or property from one person to another.

Deed: An instrument for conveying real estate.

Deed of Trust: A form of security instrument for mortgage loans.

Default: A failure to meet legal or contractual obligations.

Deficiency Judgment: When the proceeds from a foreclosure sale are less than the amount due on the debt.

Encumbrance: Any interest, right, lien, or liability attached to a parcel of land (such as unpaid taxes or an unsatisfied mortgage) that constitutes or represents a burden upon the property.

Equity: The market value of real property, less the amount of existing liens.

Escrow: Closing a real estate transaction when all required documents and funds are in place with a third party for processing and disbursement.

Execute: To sign a legal instrument. A deed is said to be executed when it is signed, sealed, witnessed, and delivered.

Federally-insured loan: A mortgage loan that originates in a federally insured government program like the Federal Housing Authority (FHA).

Foreclosure: A legal proceeding following a default by a borrower in which real estate secured by a mortgage of deed of trust is sold to satisfy the underlying debt.

Instrument: A written document.

Judgment: The decision of a court regarding the rights of parties in an action.

Junior Mortgage: A mortgage lower in lien priority than another. For example, a second mortgage or home equity line.

Lawsuit: A dispute between two or more parties than has been filed in the court system by one of them.

Lien: A monetary charge imposed on a property, usually arising from some debt or obligation.

Lis Pendens: A recorded legal notice that there is litigation pending relating to the land, and a warning that anyone obtaining an interest subsequent to the date of the notice to be bound by the judgement.

Market value: The average of the highest price that a buyer would pay and lowest price a seller would accept.

Mortgage: A conditioned pledge of property to a creditor as security for the payment of a debt.

Note (also called a Promissory Note): A written promise to pay a sum of money, usually at a specified interest rate, at a stated time to a named payee.

Power of Attorney: A written instrument by which one person, the principal, authorizes another, the attorney-in-fact, to act on his or her behalf.

Principal: A sum of money owed as a debt on which interest is payable.

Public records: Records which by law disclose constructive notice of matters relating to the land.

Real estate (also called real property): Land and anything permanently affixed to the land such as buildings, fences, and those things attached to the buildings, such as plumbing and heavy fixtures, or other such items that would be personal property if not attached.

Redemption: The right of the owner in some states to reclaim title to property if he or she pays the debt to the mortgagee within a stipulated time after foreclosure.

Release: To relieve from debt or security or abandon a right, such as release of a mortgage lien from a part or all of the land mortgaged.

RESPA: The Real Estate Settlement Procedures Act (12 U.S.C. 2601 et.seq.) that, together with Regulation X promulgated pursuant to the Act, regulates real estate transfers involving a "federally-related mortgage loan" by requiring, among other things, certain disclosures to buyers.

Satisfaction: An instrument releasing the lien of a mortgage.

Senior lien or mortgage: If there is more than one lien on land, those liens are ranked by priority. A senior lien or mortgage is entitled to be paid first in foreclosure or bankruptcy, before a junior lien.

Tenant: One who has the right of possession of land by any kind of title.

Title defect: Any possible or patent claim or right outstanding in a chain of title that is adverse to the claim of ownership.

Title insurance policy: A contract of title insurance under which the insurer, in keeping with the terms of the policy, agrees to indemnify the insured against loss arising from claims against the insured interest.

Trustee: Person or entity who is given the legal authority to manage money or property on behalf of somebody else. In a foreclosure action, this is often the title company.

Trustor: A persons who creates a trust by transferring property to a trustee. When a borrower signs the Deed of Trust, the borrower becomes a trustor.

Contacts

U.S Department of Housing and Urban Development
800-569-4287
www.hud.gov

Annual Credit Report
877-322-8228
www.annualcreditreport.com

The Center for Responsible Appraisals and Valuations
866-244-9708
www.cravonline.com

Cambridge Funding Group
949-334-6300
www.cambridgefunding.net

RealtyTrac
877-888-8722
www.RealtyTrac.com

Veterans Affairs, Home Loans
www.homeloans.va.gov

ABOUT THE AUTHORS

Bill Nazur
Mortgage Banker, Real Estate Finance Specialist, Investor

Bill Nazur boasts a 95 percent ratio of return clients in the ever-competitive mortgage industry. A key to his success lies in his ability to review and understand each client's specific needs, and customize a mortgage that will help each client satisfy their individual desires. Although he works on originating mortgage loans, Bill has a network of trusted advisors consisting of Certified Financial Planners, CPAs, real estate agents, brokers, and even other bankers, from which his clients greatly benefit. With over 20 years of experience in sales, marketing, and finance, Bill has worked with every client ranging from first-time homebuyers to the most discriminating investor, having financed over 200 clients each year for the last five consecutive years.

Bill has worked for major lending institutions, such as Bank of America, Washington Mutual, and Cambridge Funding Group as the exclusive lender to the Prudential California Realty Network, as well as in sales, marketing, and finance with Marriott and Starwood Hotels since 1987. Bill has been a multiple year President's Club recipient and Top Producer since 1989.

Bill has membership and serves in several professional organizations, such as the National Association of Hispanic Real Estate Professionals, the Pacific West Association of Realtors, and the Women's Council of Realtors of Whittier, helping hone his skills and acquire new ones in a continually changing real estate environment throughout the United States. He is also a Licensed California Real Estate Professional.

He currently resides in Corona, California.

Danielle Babb, PhD, MBA
Investor, Consultant, and Professor

Danielle Babb is a technology professional with years of experience in the real estate industry. She has worked as an IT Leader in residential, commercial, and multi-unit real estate. She has worked for seven years at several Fortune 500 real estate companies in the technology field and both consults and presents regularly on the use of technology in real estate. Danielle has a PhD in Organization and Management with a technology emphasis, as well as an MBA with a technology emphasis. She is a Licensed California Real Estate Professional.

Dr. Dani has written and presented numerous papers on technology and business and has become a specialist in the field of technology's impact on business. In particular, she's focused her work on the ever-changing real estate market and the influence technology is having on the industry. She invests in all types of real estate nationwide and brings many years of investment and consulting experience to her audiences and readers. Her experience as an educator is vital to her success as an author, with a consistent goal of educating the consumer and helping others be their best. Through this book she hopes to help people find great deals, buy their first home, or retire early—or all of the above!

She currently resides in Newport Beach, California.

INDEX

Finding Foreclosures | An Insider's Guide to Cashing In on this Hidden Market

To Our Readers,

We evaluated many foreclosures sites before selecting the one we thought would best fit your needs. RealtyTrac was hands down the best site. We then decided to contact them and invite them to review our manuscript and supply us with some additional insider information that might benefit you, our readers.

We are happy to announce that in addition to their valuable advice, RealtyTrac has also agreed to extend a special offer to our readers. We hope you take advantage of it.

—*Dani & Bill*